The Power of

Other Books
by Harrison Owen

*The Spirit of Leadership: Liberating the Leader
    in Each of Us*

Open Space Technology: A User's Guide

*Expanding Our Now: The Story of Open Space
    Technology*

*Spirit: Transformation and Development in
    Organizations*

Riding the Tiger

The Millennium Organization

Tales from Open Space

The Power of Spirit

Spirit

How Organizations Transform

Harrison Owen

BERRETT-KOEHLER PUBLISHERS, INC.
San Francisco

Berrett-Koehler Publishers, Inc.
450 Sansome Street, Suite 1200
San Francisco, CA 94111-3320
Tel: (415) 288-0260   Fax: (415) 362-2512   www.bkconnection.com

Ordering Information

Quantity sales. Special discounts are available on quantity purchases by corporations, associations, and others. For details, contact the "Special Sales Department" at the Berrett-Koehler address above.

Individual sales. Berrett-Koehler publications are available through most bookstores. They can also be ordered direct from Berrett-Koehler:
Tel: (800) 929-2929; Fax: (802) 864-7626; www.bkconnection.com

Orders for college textbook/course adoption use. Please contact Berrett-Koehler:
Tel: (800) 929-2929; Fax: (802) 864-7626.

Orders by U.S. trade bookstores and wholesalers. Please contact Publishers Group West, 1700 Fourth Street, Berkeley, CA 94710. Tel: (510) 528-1444; Fax: (510) 528-3444.

Printed in the United States of America

 Printed on acid-free and recycled paper that is composed of 50% recovered fiber, including 10% post consumer waste.

Library of Congress Cataloging-in-Publication Data

Owen, Harrison. 1935–
    The power of spirit : how organizations transform / Harrison Owen.
      p. cm.
    Includes bibliographical references and index.
    ISBN 1-57675-090-6 (alk. paper)
    1. Organizational change. 2.Organizational effectiveness 3. Communication in organizations. I. Title.

    HD58.8.O938 2000
    658.4'06--dc21
                                            00-031158

First Edition

06 05 04 03 02 01 00   10 9 8 7 6 5 4 3 2 1

Design: Gopa Design   Proofread: Henrietta Bensussen
Edit: Elinor Lindheimer   Index: Paula C. Durbin-Westby
Production: Linda Jupiter, Jupiter Productions

Table of Contents

Preface

THIS BOOK COMPLETES the Open Space Quartet. *Expanding Our Now* introduces Open Space Technology. *Open Space Technology: A User's Guide* provides the essential "how to" information. *The Spirit of Leadership* explores the nature and function of leadership in an open space environment, where control as we used to know it has ceased to exist. This present book completes the story by providing the critical link between a meeting methodology and a very new way of being in organization.

All of these books, with the exception of *Expanding Our Now*, had a previous life with Abbott Publishing. Thanks to Steve Piersanti and the good people at Berrett-Koehler, they are now available to a much broader audience, usually with major revision and additions. This book is no exception, and while some of the thoughts and words began life in my earlier books (*Spirit: Transformation and Development in Organizations, Riding the Tiger, The Millennium Organization,* and *Tales from Open Space*), this is not simply a rehash of what has gone before. There is much new material and new ways of looking at older ideas. My intent is to offer a distillation of 40 years of thinking about and working in organizations of all sorts.

Harrison Owen
Potomac, Maryland
June 2000

Prologue:
Spirit Is the Most Important Thing

THIS BOOK IS ABOUT SPIRIT, and the ways in which Spirit forms and transforms in organizations. It is written from the belief, and experience, that Spirit is the most important thing. When the Spirit of a people is strong, focused, and vibrant, wonderful things can happen. When the Spirit is down, it makes very little difference how good your reputation, how much money you have in the bank, or how strong the need for your goods or services. Not too much happens.

There are two sorts of people who may find this book of interest. First, those who have come to realize that the Spirit in their place of work, to say nothing of their own Spirit, is getting a little tattered, showing the early stages of what I call Soul Pollution. These indicators include a certain apathy when it comes to going to work, a recognition that the last time you had fun on the job was when you quit, a tendency to feel overwhelmed by the great amorphous *They*. Those in the advanced stages of Soul Pollution, characterized by exhaustion, high levels of stress, and the abuse of just about anything in sight, including spouses, substances, and fellow workers, may be especially interested.

For all sufferers of Soul Pollution, the message of the book is this: Things do not have to be this bad. In fact, we are shooting ourselves in the foot, and there is indeed a better way. We need only stop holding on to some questionable beliefs, accept ourselves as we are, and get on with the business of living. It is just that simple. The details and the fine points may be complex, and we will be exploring a number of those fine complexities. And getting from here to there may *seem* an impossible leap. But in truth the "fix" is no big deal. Just do it.

There is another, much smaller, group of people who will find this book of interest. This group includes those intrepid souls who have ventured into the realm of Open Space Technology, and who may be wondering what to do next. After a great meeting, is that all there is? My answer is an emphatic No! It is only the beginning. What has been experienced in Open Space can be a 365-day-a-year reality.

So what is the secret? Create some space. Open the doors and windows of your life and organizations. Move the walls, and let Spirit show up. Keep that space open and Soul Pollution dissipates as Spirit perks up—*provided* our faulty notions of control are put aside. So whether you are an Open Space Technology practitioner or you've never heard of such a strange thing, but find yourself dreading another day on the job in an organization seemingly bent on its own destruction as well as the destruction of its members, I invite you to read on.

OPENING SPACE FOR SPIRIT

Opening space for Spirit, as in High Spirit, Playful Spirit, Productive Spirit, is not (or certainly *not only*) an esoteric undertaking. Indeed, it can become a practical everyday experience for those who care to try. One approach, and only one approach, is what is now called Open Space Technology.

Open Space Technology[1] is a simple means for the facilitation of complex human endeavors. In a typical situation, 500 people assemble to plot the future course of their institution. The diversity of the group is enormous and the signs of conflict are everywhere apparent. Prior to this meeting, absolutely no advance planning has been done relative to the agenda. The group sits in a large circle, and there is one facilitator. In less than 20 minutes the facilitator has concluded his remarks, and the group moves to productive work. Forty-five minutes later, every issue of concern that anybody in the group thought to raise has been placed on the table, or more accurately posted on a previously blank wall that has now become a huge bulletin board. There are 140 postings, each with an assigned time, place of meeting, and a designated convener. Half an hour later, all participants have signed up for the groups of their choosing and are hard at work. For two days the group as a whole self-manages the task. Forty-eight hours from start there are 500 bound copies of proceedings (350 pages each) available to all participants as they go home.

The manifest behaviors of the group are of equal note. Self-managed work teams are the norm. Leadership appears when and as needed. Conflict pops up, but typically resolves into positive solutions, unaided by outside assistance. Diversity of opinion is honored and built upon. Stress levels are at an all time low—and perhaps best of all—many people describe the whole affair as fun.

It appears that there is a way to achieve high levels of productive work with minimum stress, nonproductive conflict, and exhaustion. It is even possible to have fun at work. If this can happen for two days— why not all the time?

Had the meeting described been a "once and only" phenomenon, one might suspect incredible good luck. However, what happened with that group has been repeated thousands of times all over the world. And the results have been the same. Indeed, Open Space works very well in any organization with a burning issue, characterized by the following: high levels of complexity, diversity, and conflict (actual or potential); and with a decision time of yesterday. Open Space does not work, and should not be used, in any situation where the answers are already known, the outcomes predetermined, and/or where someone has determined that it is essential to be in charge and maintain control.

THE OPEN SPACE EXPERIMENT

In the 15 years since the first Open Space gathering, the experience for me has moved out of the realm of interesting occurrence to become a natural experiment in which to explore the untapped possibilities of our common humanity.

As an experiment, it should commence with a clear hypothesis, precisely stated experimental conditions and definable procedures, and be repeatable with predictable results, irrespective of the experimenter (facilitator).[2] The hypothesis is: *concerned human beings, gathering of their own free will, and regardless of social status, education, ethnicity, or economics, can quickly [almost instantaneously] create effective organization productive of substantive results, without extensive preparation and massive amounts of external assistance.*

The experimental conditions are as noted above: high levels of complexity, diversity, and conflict (actual or potential), with a decision time of yesterday. The procedures are: sit in a circle, create a bulletin board, open a marketplace, and get on with the business. To date, and so far as I know, every time the conditions have been met and the procedures followed, the hypothesis has been confirmed.

SELF-ORGANIZATION: THE SECRET OF OPEN SPACE

So what is the secret? The answer, at least in part, comes from what we are now learning about self-organizing systems. According to a growing number of researchers, systems organize all by themselves, provided certain essential preconditions are met. For the most part such research has concentrated on physical and biological systems. The Open Space experiment suggests that a similar phenomenon also occurs with human systems, such as businesses, governments, and other sorts of collections of people. And best of all, the result is productive and stimulating—even joyful and fun. Now there is an antidote for Soul Pollution, a way to rally sagging Spirit, and still get the job done.

A TRANSFORMATIVE MOMENT

If it all works so well, and feels so good, why are we still so hesitant? I believe the answer is simple. Should we take the necessary step there is the strong possibility—indeed the absolute certainty—that things will get out of control. Even worse, it will become apparent to us that the control we thought we had was but a fond delusion.[3]

When told about the happenings in Open Space, many people respond that it all seems so counter-intuitive, a polite way of saying that it is impossible and probably wrong. We all know, as a matter of the basic understanding of human nature, that 500 angry, confused people with no prepared agenda and minimal facilitation will produce catastrophe. Why would we want to go there?

But should it turn out that this basic understanding about ourselves was in error, it would seem reasonable to find a new self-understanding. Vastly easier to say than do.

Giving up our basic self-understanding in favor of a new one, particularly one that seems very risky to say nothing of impossible and even wrong, is a very scary thing. It is all about transformation—which is never to be taken lightly. It means, quite literally, that we will become new people, that our Spirit will show up in a new way.

So here we sit: a bumper crop of Soul Pollution and growing evidence that our organizations are becoming less functional and more destructive. There must be a better way!

It is indeed a transformative moment. It is a time of choosing, and I believe the choice is ours. More of the same old, same old . . . or something very new. We are on a journey.

The purpose of this book is to trace that journey. We will point out some of the pitfalls and possibilities, suggest ways to make the passage more productive, if not easier, and then offer a first approximation of what our new life might be like, including the essential skills and modes of operation necessary for survival. Indeed more than survival, for I fully believe that we are entering upon a phase of human existence that will positively blow away our prior conceptions of what it means to be *Homo sapiens*. Of course there are no guarantees, and it may be that we will blow the whole trip. However, as a species we have done fairly well to the present, and it is just possible that we will muddle through.

A WORD ABOUT THE AUTHOR,
THE SOURCES, AND THE APPROACH

Before beginning our journey it is probably useful for you to know something about me, the sources I draw from, and the overall approach. *Caveat emptor* if you will.

I am an Anglican Priest, or Episcopalian as it would be known in the United States. I fully intended to be an academic with areas of interest including the myth, ritual, and culture of the ancient Near East, particularly as these elements gave expression to an understanding of chaos, order, and the creative process.

That career was trashed in the middle 1960s with the Birmingham bombings and the emergence of the civil rights struggle. I traded library stacks for city streets as I participated in, and organized, a variety of civil rights activities. Over the next 15 years I found myself in the role of executive director of a large community association in Washington, D.C., a member of the Peace Corps staff in West Africa, director of a large health care infrastructure building program on Long Island, ending up back in Washington at the National Institutes of Health, and ultimately at the Veterans Administration as a political appointee in the Carter administration.

For the next 20 years, I had the privilege of working as a consultant with an incredible range of organizations and institutions, including corporations, small villages, street gangs, and political institutions, on virtually every continent and subcontinent on the planet.

The sources for this book are quite simply my life experience—all of it. This means that we will be visiting some possibly strange places, ranging from esoteric literature to contemporary chaos and complexity theory, all the while seeking reference and grounding in the everyday working world.

The thoughts of many people, ancient and modern, have been formative for me, and I will acknowledge those contributions as we proceed. But this is not an academic treatise, and I am not a scholar. Artist, poet, or storyteller would be a closer fit.

To be truthful, storyteller is probably the best representation of how I work. I acknowledge that storytellers are suspect and more than occasionally have a light regard for the facts. But good storytellers do infinitely more than render the facts. Their profession and their art is to weave a tale out of the threads of common experience to the end that an imaginative space and time is created in which teller and listener collaboratively may perceive new truth about old facts.

If the idea of dealing with a storyteller is not to your liking, try theory builder instead. For in truth a theory is "only" a likely story that assembles available facts in a coherent fashion so that they may be understood, and useful work accomplished. Asking whether a theory is true or false is to fundamentally misunderstand the nature of theory. The real question is: does the theory work, and can it account for current events and predict future occurrences?

Whether you think of me as a storyteller or theoretician, it is all the same. The final question for me is: does it work?

IT'S ALL ABOUT SPIRIT

You will have noticed that I use the word Spirit quite a lot. And not just with a small "s," but with a capital letter, as in Spirit. This is not simply an affectation, but comes from a deep conviction that Spirit is the most important "thing" in any organization.

I have not tried to define Spirit, but I don't believe that is really possible; at least I have never been very successful. More to the point, I am not at all sure that definition is necessary. We all know Spirit when we meet it. In its presence there is excitement, innovation, what we might call inspired performance. And *inspiration*, after all, literally means to "in-Spirit."

I will use the word Spirit undefined, and you may think about it in any way that works for you. That might be team spirit, *esprit de corps,* high spirits, deep spirit, or even the eternal Spirit—the mother of us all. From where I sit, all these are connected. Start at any one point, and you will eventually arrive at all the rest. If you must have a definition, then you might think of this whole book as that definition, for this book is all about Spirit, and the ways in which Spirit forms and transforms in the organizations of our world.

There is also a theoretical reason why I spend so much time on Spirit. A major theme of this work is transformation in organizations. When the subject is transformation, the word itself tells us that we are dealing with a process in which something (unnamed) goes through, or across, forms—trans-forms, as it were. The focus is not on the forms, which is what most people talk about, but rather that which goes through the forms, which is what I think we *should* be talking about. And that "something," so far as I am concerned, is Spirit. Of course it is hard to see Spirit, but we can certainly see its footprints. Following those footprints is the nub of our story. All the rest is pretty much window dressing.

PREVIEW OF THE STORY: THE FORMATION AND TRANSFORMATION OF SPIRIT IN ORGANIZATIONS

The story is told in four parts. Part I, *Chaos, Order, and Self-Organizing Systems,* faces the beast in its lair: chaos, and the terrible possibility that things might get out of control. It turns out, however, that chaos is never really avoidable, and thank goodness for that. For chaos, and the disequilibrium it brings, is an essential condition for life, learning, innovation, and—strange as it may seem—organization. At least the sort of organization that appears through self-organization, which some people call a Complex Adaptive System.

Such a system is *complex,* in that it has multiple elements, *adaptive,* in that it continually changes to fit the environment, and a *system,* in that it is organized. The odd thing is that nobody did the organizing. The system did it all by itself, or as Stuart Kauffman[4] of the Santa Fe Institute would say, "Order for Free."

Complex Adaptive Systems come in all shapes and sizes, from a molecular stew up to human organizations and beyond to the cosmos itself. Held in common are certain basic and necessary preconditions for self-organization, which initiate and sustain the process. But humans are also different from rocks and molecules. Humans usually know that something is going on, and have certain feelings about it. They also have choice. Therefore the process of adaptation in human systems has certain additional elements.

These differences are considered in Part II, entitled *Transformation: The Adaptive Process in Human Systems.* The process of self-organization starts, or restarts, when chaos strikes. Suddenly the old tried and true ways don't work any more, and the choice is either cash in the chips or find a new way of doing things. For human beings this is a painful experience, involving letting go of the old ways and venturing out into something totally new. Very nervous-making. But there is a way through and we have done it many times. It is called Griefwork, or more accurately Grief-at-work. As grief works, the human system has the possibility (but not a guarantee) of adapting to the changed environment, and appearing in a new form appropriate to the new challenges. Knowledge of the Griefwork process is more than an interesting academic incidental. If you know what is happening, there is a higher likelihood of actually getting through it all.

In Part III we take a look at the ways in which Spirit shows up in emergent organizational forms. Human systems go through evolutionary development, beginning with the simple and proceeding to the more complex. There are many ways one might characterize this sequence. Mine is: ReActive, Responsive, ProActive, InterActive, and Inspired.

To give you something of the flavor, a ReActive Organization is the brash young start-up, home to the entrepreneur. It is exciting, vital, juicy—but it has little time for customers, who always seem to be getting in the way. The Responsive Organization takes care of its customers, but in a simplistic, almost pedantic way. This is a comfortable organization, but very shortsighted when it comes to rational planning and the finer points of management. A ProActive Organization is what every well-managed organization has hoped to be, until fairly recently, where control is the most important thing, and chaos is the enemy.

Under the best of circumstances this is a well-oiled machine, doing everything by the numbers. It is home to the MBA. But the good old ProActive Organization is getting very tired. The harder it tries to gain control, the more control slips through its fingers, yielding frustration, burnout, and Soul Pollution. Something has to give.

Next up is the InterActive Organization, which actually enjoys chaos. Hidden in the orderly patterns of disorder are new opportunities and the possibility of learning constantly. Work and play are synonymous and productivity simply boggles the mind. This is a conscious self-organizing system.

Lastly there is the Inspired Organization. We really don't know too much about this, but we have some hints, as when a research team goes so far beyond its known technical capacity that it seems to be floating in inspiration. This doesn't happen often, but when it does, people never forget.

So much for the schema, now for the point. It is my belief that we are uncomfortably perched between the ProActive Organization and the InterActive Organization. We know increasingly that the old ways aren't working as well as they used to, and in some cases not working at all. And we can pretty well see the future, but we do not like the ticket of admission, which is quite simply to give up the increasingly absurd notion that we are, or should be, in total control. So we sit on the fence, and fence-sitting hurts.

But while we sit, summoning the courage to let go and move on, I think a very strange and wonderful thing is happening. Without our effort, and in spite of our fears, the transformation is taking place. I can't prove it, but I think there are some good signs, good enough in fact that we can spend some profitable time thinking through what it will mean to live in an InterActive Organization, and what are some of the new skills necessary to support our new lifestyle.

Part IV makes the jump. This one is called *Cultivating Spirit: The Care and Feeding of the InterActive Organization*. Our interests there will range from some creative uses of the Internet to the arcane art of myth-making, ending with a few critical thoughts about ethics and values.

part

Chaos, Order, and
Self-Organizing Systems

CHAOS AND ORDER. An antithesis if there ever was one. In the presence of chaos, order takes a holiday. And order, of course, is the essential antidote for all that is chaotic. More than simple word games, however, the opposition of chaos and order takes on the proportions of the primordial mythic struggle between good and evil, light and darkness. To be on the side of order is to be on the side of right, truth, God. As for chaos, that is the domain of the devil and all his, or her, works of darkness.

On more mundane levels, the struggle between chaos and order continues. A chaotic life is to be avoided, and businesses that experience massive amounts of chaos are typically not good investments. And the key to victory is control.

Throughout history and even recently, those who take charge and exercise the maximum degree of control are the heroes and heroines of our world. From the executive suite to the flood plains of the Mississippi, the person who controls is worthy of our respect. A take-charge attitude, combined with the capacity to execute, has been a sure ticket to the corner office on the top floor. And down along the riverbanks, The Corps of Army Engineers heroically battled the mighty Mississippi into submission, all in the name of Flood Control. Or so they said.

But the mind-boggling complexity of global business has rendered micromanagement (total control) at the macro level quite absurd. And of course, the mighty Mississippi has had some nasty messages for those who really thought she could be controlled.

What if control, as we have thought about it, is delusion, and chaos, despite its unpleasant aspects, is essential for life?

What if—indeed.

chapter 1

Chaos and the End of Control
As We Knew It

IF THERE IS A SINGLE SACRED WORD in the culture of most of our organizations, that word is control. When we have it, we are in good shape, and in its absence disaster is a short step away.

As managers we have been trained to control, and control is the prime attribute designating high-quality management. The centrality of control is not usually stated so blatantly, but it is never far from the surface. According to the old dictum, the good manager makes the plan, manages to the plan, and meets the plan. And the essence of all of that is control. Close, tight control.

We presently find ourselves in rather strange circumstances. It remains relatively easy to make a plan, for after all we control the pen, paper, or computer. But ensuring that the plan, once made, will have any relevance past the drying of its ink, is no easy task. Sure as the sun rises, some unpredicted event will shatter our best efforts. These are hard days for plan makers, and all those other folks who place high value on being in control.

But what are the options? Somewhere along the line we came to the conclusion that the only alternative to control was being out of control. And we all know what that means. Chaos!

In the good old days (whenever they were), events moved at a stately pace, allowing us to make our plans with some reasonable hope of completion. And indeed, we often looked forward to a little chaos just for added spice. Chaos is no longer a little spice added to the organizational stew. It has become our daily bread and butter. As Mikhail Gorbachev said, "We are already in a state of chaos." (*Washington Post*, Fall 1990) Maybe someday we can return to normal.

SOMEDAY WILL NEVER COME

The hope for a return to normalcy is precluded by myriad factors. I will mention only two: first, the state of the planet; and second, the electronic connection.

The State of the Planet

It is not my intention to deliver an impassioned plea for ecological reform, although that is certainly in order. Rather I merely wish to point to the present sorry state of the planet as a prime factor precluding any possible return to normalcy. Take whatever list of ecological disasters you wish (present, imminent, or potential), and it is patently obvious to even the casual observer that the base system, upon which all other systems stand, is badly out of whack, and showing every sign of becoming more so. Acid rain, global warming, depletion of the ozone layer, destruction of the planetary lungs (rain forests), toxic wastes, are just examples of the many ecological problems; it seems almost pointless to count them. Each contributes, and all conspire, to create the conditions under which we will never return to normal, and business as usual. For it was "business as usual" that got us into this mess.

The productive capacity of the West—now spread around the world—has indeed been good business. However it is business as usual, which is about to put all of us out of business. Scientific studies documenting the appearance of the Greenhouse Effect combined with predictions of the ultimate outcomes are sufficient to give you nightmares.

And the nightmare is quickly becoming a "daymare" as our once crystalline blue skies smudge over with the noxious fumes of millions of automobiles, factories, and power plants. Worse, an unsightly mess has become a genuine hazard to our health. In Bombay, Mexico City, Los Angeles, to say nothing of Washington, D.C., pollution alerts are now a way of life, and evacuations of the young and old a growing occurrence. Truly, it is getting hard to breathe, and as any business person understands full well, customers who stop breathing are rather unlikely to buy. In a word, getting back to normal, or returning to business as usual, is a one-way ticket to disaster. We really don't want to go there.

The Electronic Connection

Not terribly long ago, the notion that our planet was a small electronic cottage appeared "far out" and avant-garde. However, science fiction is now an everyday experience. We are all connected and virtually instantaneously. When something happens in a far corner of the planet, we know it, and react. What all of this has to do with the impossibility of returning to "normal" is quite simple. Our organizations and institutions, almost without exception, were designed for a much different era, and even those human systems designed most recently are apparently patterned on what has gone before.

The archetype for organization design emerged early in the 1900s, a classic period in the United States with the organization of General Motors, DuPont, Standard Oil of New Jersey, and Sears and Roebuck. Chronicled by Alfred Chandler[1] these corporations manifested organizational charts of such complex precision as to boggle the mind. Presumably all of this worked, and certainly everything was most impressive on paper. But that was a slower, simpler day and we could afford to pursue the majestic process—up and down the organization chart. But control was optimized and order prevailed, or so it is said in the textbooks.

As we know all too well, such a majestic process is simply trashed when responsive decisions must be made in minutes and not months or years. The net result is that decisions are not made or are made poorly and late, or the participants simply gasp with exhaustion. Stress and burnout become a seemingly inescapable cost of doing business.

More recently the insanity of the situation has been acknowledged, and major efforts have been launched to reduce organizational layers, and thereby enhance the efficiency of the process. But the fundamental understanding of the nature of organization remains unchanged. To be sure, layers have been reduced, but the essential design remains the same. It is still made up of layers, albeit fewer of them.

It would seem that the lessons of chaos and complexity have yet to be learned. Or if they have been learned at a conceptual level, they are not yet assimilated at a deeper level, where a fundamental change in understanding takes place. The notion remains that someday, somehow, we will create the perfect structure that will ensure the continuance of control. Surely somebody is in charge, if only we could find the right person and the right structure. Lots of luck.

GUESS WHAT? THIS IS NORMAL. CHAOS IS A NATURAL PART OF LIFE

Slowly it is dawning on most of us: there is no going back, and what we now experience is normal. If this is so, then perhaps chaos is not antithetical to life, but rather a normal, natural, and possibly necessary aspect of what it means to be alive.

Not very long ago such a thought was pure heresy, for have we not all been taught that the lack of order is the end of productive existence? Science, at least as we learned it in school, had one basic message: the universe is an orderly place, thus the scientific method and prediction are possible. From Newton onward, we have lived in a clockwork universe with a time and place for everything, and everything in its peculiar time and place. Were things to get out of order, it was the role of science to put it back together. Maybe.

Of course, some other aspects of the scientific endeavor do not appear to play by the same rules. Subatomic physics, for example, has found itself in world of randomness where indeterminacy is the rule, if a rule can be indeterminate. However, this may all have been an aberration, and such a luminary as Albert Einstein boldly proclaimed, "God does not play dice." For Einstein, as for many of us, the thought of a fundamentally disorderly universe is appalling. Little storms and small disturbances to be sure—but chaos as a natural part of life?

A WORD FROM THE PAST

Actually, the thought that chaos is not only a natural aspect of life, but an essential and positive element, is not a new one. So far as I am aware, every major religious tradition has held this view. Of course, that does not make it true, but at least it may give us pause for thought.

For the Hindu, Shiva, the Lord of the Universe, is usually depicted with two faces. One of the faces is that of the creator. But the second is the face of destruction and chaos. The picture is relatively clear. The universe is the product of an alternation, or better, a synergy of forces: order and disorder, cosmos and chaos.

From a different part of the globe comes a similar thought. The Taoist tradition of China places much weight on the yin and the yang. While often thought of as male and female polarities, there is in fact a deeper meaning. The yin and the yang can equally refer to the light and the dark, the forces of order and the breakthrough of chaos. If life were all order, there could be no evolution. Were it all chaos, there could be no continuance. It is only in the dance between chaos and order that life progresses.

The interplay of the powers of chaos and order, as an expression of the divine intent, finds its place also in Judaism. The sacred history of the people of Israel may be read as a guided passage through chaos and on to New Creation (to use the phrase from Jeremiah). From Egypt, into the chaos of the Desert, and on to the Promised Land. But note: the Desert is the antechamber to the Promised Land. The prophet Isaiah[2] puts the thought quite directly when he says (speaking for God), "I create the Light and make the Darkness. I create peace (*shalom*) and chaos (*tohu w' bohu*)."

In Christianity, the centrality of chaos in the process of existence is clearly stated through the stark symbolism of the cross. In the language of that faith, crucifixion stands as an intermediary between life and new life (Resurrection). Christmas, Good Friday, then Easter—that is the story.

Is all of this true? Who knows? But that is the story, and it is a story that has been told in the community of humanity with remarkable consistency for a very long time. It is only in the recent past (since the dawn of the scientific age) that we have attempted to tell a different story, in which disorder and chaos are banished from the universe as aberrant and fundamentally useless phenomena. Perhaps our new story is the aberrancy?

A WORD FROM THE PRESENT

History now seems to be repeating itself, or perhaps we are now remembering what we have tried very hard to forget. Science, or at least some scientific disciplines, has now rediscovered chaos. Within the past thirty years, from a very broad spectrum of scientific disciplines, there has emerged first a suspicion, and now something that looks remarkably like a coherent body of knowledge, all gathered under the umbrella of chaos theory. I leave it to James Gleick[3] and others to describe the details, but in a nutshell, the chaos theorists are proposing that not only is there a pattern in chaos, but that chaos is useful.

The pattern emerges upon consideration of the life cycle of any natural, open system. Open systems are to be contrasted with closed systems, which turn out to be figments of our imagination, existing only as theoretical constructs, albeit useful ones for the conduct of science.

For example, if one were to seek some strange new electronic particle, it is essential to "wall out" interference from all other particles that might get in the way of the experiment. At a practical level, walls of lead and concrete are constructed to protect the experimental environment (close the system), but even with best efforts it is never quite possible to achieve the tight, hermetical seal that might be hoped for. The next part is an act of hope, and probably also faith. Everybody hopes that such elements that do break through will create a level of disturbance so low as might be disregarded. Thus even in the laboratory environment, where scientists do their best to "close the system" and thereby control the unwanted variables, something always seems to get through. It may just be an aberrant neutron, with an impact so small as to be forgettable, but something opens the can.

There is a lesson for managers in all of this scientific jargon. We have been treating our organizations as if they were closed systems, which we might fully control—all under the heading of scientific management. The truth of the matter is that all systems are open, and most especially our organizations. Is it any wonder that efforts to control inevitably meet with disappointment?

Now back to chaos. When you observe the process of a natural system, it is noted that the life cycle is punctuated by periods of order and chaos. Sometimes things go right, and sometimes we are in deep tapioca. There is no news here, but a definable, predictable pattern emerges. While one may not be able to say when this pattern will begin or end, that it will occur is assured.

The pattern divides into four stages. The first stage might be called Steady State with Development. Everything is going along fine, and getting better. The second stage is called Periodic Doubling, the meaning of which we will come to shortly. In the third stage, chaos appears, which means that all previous patterns are broken and predictability becomes a thing of the past. The final stage may have one of two forms: dissolution, or renewal at a higher order of complexity. The meaning of dissolution should be obvious: everything falls apart, and it is over.[4]

Renewal at a higher order of complexity is the intriguing piece. Somehow this Open System gets itself back together, not as it was, but in a new (usually radically new) fashion, which is at the same time related to its past (it is still recognizably the same sort of thing), *and* in synergistic harmony with the new environment.

For example, suppose that our Open System is a population of deer. Each year the males and females do what they are supposed to do, and the herd increases. We might say that the herd is stable and getting better, and predictably, given sufficient water and food, things will only improve.

But one year a very strange thing happens. For absolutely no observable reason, the number of births doubles. The next year, the number of births is halved. And so it continues for a few years, doubling up and then doubling down (this is Periodic Doubling). After a time, and usually a very short time, any logic or rationale in the number of births totally disappears, and we have chaos. From that point on one of two possibilities will come to pass. Either the herd will disappear from the face of the earth, or it will restabilize in some new functional pattern, more conducive to living in its environment.

The critical point was the onset of Periodic Doubling, and the critical question is, why did it occur? Here we must introduce the butterfly. One of the most profound discoveries of the chaos theorists is that *Open Systems have extreme sensitivity to early conditions*. Translated, that means that sometime in the early life of the herd something happened or didn't happen. At the time, this happening would have appeared so trivial as to be inconsequential. But somehow the impact of this happening was carried along in the life of the herd in a dormant state. Suddenly, for no apparent reason, the happening happens again, the balance is tripped, and Periodic Doubling commences. Now back to the butterfly. It is part of the folklore of chaos theorists that a butterfly flapping its wings in Thailand will affect the weather system of California. Who knows whether it is true, and it is doubtful that the butterfly will ever be caught in the act. But that is the story.

WHAT EARTHLY GOOD IS CHAOS?

If chaos has a place in the natural order of things, it seems pertinent to ask, does it do any good? Has it any use, and if so, what?

Arnold Mandell, quoted in Gleick's book, poses the question in an interesting and provocative manner. "Is it not possible that mathematical pathology, i.e., chaos, is health? And that mathematical health, which is predictability . . . is disease?" He then says pointedly: "When you reach an equilibrium in biology, you're dead."[5]

The suggestion is that chaos represents the growth point in any system. Or in a term that we will be using rather extensively, chaos creates the *Open Space* in which the new can emerge. Obviously there are no guarantees here, for chaos can equally mark the end—in fact it always does. The central question is not about ending, but rather the possibility of new beginning. Chaos may therefore be the essential precondition for all that is truly new. No chaos, nothing new.

One of the unique aspects of chaos in my experience (and I suspect everybody else's) is *difference*. Whatever else may be true, the chaotic situation is different, unlike what preceded it and what follows. We may not like the difference, and indeed that difference may be downright painful. But there is no denying that there is a difference.

Gregory Bateson[6] teaches us that the perception of difference is the essence of learning. Or in his words, learning occurs when we notice "differences that make a difference." This deceptively simple phrase takes us in interesting directions, for it suggests, in the present context, that the function of chaos is to create the conditions in which real learning can take place.

While it may be true that chaos is part of the life story of all systems, our concern here is primarily human systems—practical concerns like businesses, governments, and other organizations, productive of the goods and services we as human beings require. Furthermore, the pressure of the moment makes it essential that we focus our attention not on the maintenance of what is, but on the evolution of what must be if we as a species are to continue in some useful way on this planet. Learning, in its deepest sense, appears to be critical. Thus if chaos creates difference, and difference enables learning, may it not be that our nemesis is also, and simultaneously, our salvation?

So what good is chaos? Provisionally, let me propose that chaos creates the differences that make a difference, through which we learn.

chapter 2
Chaos and Learning

THE SUGGESTION THAT CHAOS AND LEARNING are naturally linked, and more, that one forms the essential precondition of the other, may appear nothing short of lunacy. Do we not know, as only countless hours in the schoolroom can teach, that learning requires order? What else does the teacher do but maintain order in the classroom so that learning may take place?

But do we not also know, as only a squirming fifth grader can know, that such order, even in mild doses (to say nothing of extreme application), can become exquisitely boring? Boring to the point that learning and boredom are often equated. It somehow seems that if we are not painfully bored, we can't be learning.

I can claim no expertise in the art and science of educating fifth graders, but I can bear testimony to my own experience of that time under the iron hand of Mr. Birdsil. Mr. Birdsil's class was the very model of order. We sat in neat rows and spoke only when spoken to, and then only rarely. Mostly we listened while Mr. Birdsil pontificated on a variety of subjects, the impact of which was so minimal as to be insignificant. Occasionally, perhaps more than occasionally, the endless pontificating would be interrupted by the abusive denunciation of some unfortunate who had fallen asleep. More usually, the denunciation was nonverbal, taking instead the form of a well-placed shot with a blackboard eraser at the sleeping head.

I do, however, remember one significant event. I had a question, and following the required procedure, I raised my hand. When recognized, I began the ritual phrase, "Mr. Birdsil . . . " But instead of "Birdsil," what came out of my mouth was "Birdseed." I am sure the devil made me do it, for I have no consciousness at all of thinking such an outrageous thought. But there it was, hanging in the shocked silence of the awestruck classroom. Mr. Birdsil looked as if the devil himself had put in an unwanted appearance, and carefully laying his chalk and eraser on the desk, he strode with ominous purpose until he towered over me. His face was white with anger except for a little red spot on the tip of his nose, which apparently came from spirit of a different sort. Then he spoke—bellowed would be more accurate—"Owen . . . what did you say?" And before I could even think of a reply, he struck me full force with an open hand in the face. I do remember that. Indeed, that may be the only learning remaining with me from the fifth grade.

Say what you will, my encounter with Mr. Birdsil was different, and in that difference came learning. Not of the best sort perhaps, but learning nonetheless. Fortunately, the balance of my educational career was not a replication of the fifth-grade experience. I came to know that learning, excitement, enthusiasm, and inspiration could all go together. But mostly what I came to know is that learning takes place when difference is perceived. Gregory Bateson was right, the essence of learning is differences that make a difference.

We need not encounter the Birdsils of the world to see Bateson's point. The deep learning moments of our lives should sufficiently make the case. A friend of mine, V.S. Mahesh,[1] made a study of such deep learning moments, and his findings, I think, are quite relevant here. He asked a large group of people (3,000 I believe) to think back to those moments in their lives when they really learned something powerful. Not an academic detail like quadratic equations, but something of deep significance, such as who I am anyhow. Then with that moment in mind he asked them to remember:

- ▼ How it felt as they were inching up to that critical time.
- ▼ What it was like in the midst of the moment.
- ▼ How it felt afterwards.

All the people answered the questions with some variant of the following: Prior to the moment of powerful learning there was a general feeling of dis-ease, what the Germans might call *angst,* which is usually translated as "anxiety," but anxiety of a sort with no particular point of reference: something is happening/going to happen out there and I don't know what it is. In the moment it was experienced as total confusion: chaos. Nothing made sense and everything was strange and different. Once the moment had passed, there was a feeling of relief at a minimum, and more typically triumph. The world, although superficially the same, was very different. Profound learning had taken place, made all too clear in the radical perception of difference.

You needn't take my word nor that of Mahesh. Try the experiment yourself. And when you do I think you will validate the presence and value of chaos in the learning experience, at least in a profound learning experience. It is all about the differences that make a difference.

MUST WE GO ALL THE WAY TO CHAOS?

If learning occurs when differences make a difference, do we have to go all the way to chaos in order to achieve the desired effect? Unfortunately, I think we do, especially in moments of deep learning. But the necessary chaos need not be of the magnitude of a major hurricane. If that were the case, learning of any useful sort would be a very rare phenomenon. In fact I think we are coming to understand that chaos is our constant companion, even though contemporary usage tends to reserve the word for those megabuster situations where everything hits the fan. There is some perceived value in this definition. By using chaos to refer only to situations of ultimate disaster, we can see our lives as being largely without chaos. And that is a great comfort. But that is also a loss.

The loss is incurred by limiting chaos to the more or less extreme cases, blinding us to a truth: everything is a question of scale,[2] and therefore a matter of perspective. Put rather more directly, my chaos can be your minor inconvenience, and vice versa. It all depends on where you sit.

For example, if you as company president conclude that one product line has become unprofitable and therefore must be terminated, that is a minor, everyday business decision for you. However if I am the maker of that product, having defined my past, present, and future in terms of its production, I will see the matter in a rather different light. For me it is chaos.

With an "absolute" definition, we are forced to think in terms of order or chaos, when it is probably more appropriate to think of order *and* chaos, the two constantly in interaction at all levels of scale. In other words, there is never a moment when we do not have chaos heading toward order, or the other way around.

NORMAL LEARNING AND HIGH LEARNING

I am sure there is a place for the ordered classroom. That is the place for Normal Learning, where we ingest all the details, facts, figures, and minutiae needed to get along with life. All of that is necessary, but hardly sufficient. Unless there is some reasonable dose of what I would like to call High Learning, life moves along with monochromatic sameness.

The notions of Normal Learning and High Learning are borrowed (with some alteration) from Thomas Kuhn.[3] Kuhn actually talks about High Science and Normal Science. The former occurs at those moments of paradigm shift, when an old way of conceptualizing the world passes before a new one appears in what is usually a tumultuous, painful event. Normal Science is what occurs after the new paradigm arrives—cleaning up the territory, so to speak.

It is but a small jump, I think, from High Science to High Learning, with only slightly different words for the same thing. Actually *science* comes from the Latin word "to know," which presumably is what learning is all about. But not all of us are scientists, and therefore we may miss the point. So I prefer the use of the more generic term *learning*. We all learn, but not all of us are Einsteins.

High Learning occurs when chaos cracks the established order, permitting us to see some difference that makes a difference. We find ourselves on a quantum leap past, and through, what we knew before, and on to a new way of perceiving the world. The chaos in question may be minimal as the world may see it, but it is sufficient to open vistas. The issue is always "sufficiency," and never some absolute quantity. After all, butterflies flapping their wings scarcely qualify as mega-events. Normal Learning is what we do after we make the perceptual leap. At some level it amounts to taking stock of the new territory.

THE GIFT OF CHAOS: INNOVATION

Innovation is the gift of chaos, appropriated by High Learning, and made useful through Normal Learning. That rather bald statement encapsulates what I understand to be the central benefit of chaos for our organizations and businesses. Although extreme in appearance, that statement may also make some sense out of the strange phenomenon that all major breakthroughs (no matter how defined) always seem to occur "by mistake," which is a polite way of talking about chaos. I know this is not the way things are supposed to happen, for we would all like to think that our advancement proceeds along an ordered course, well thought out in advance, and definitely according to plan.

A classic case is the discovery of penicillin and with it, the advent of the so-called miracle drugs. According to the story, we never would have had this wonder drug if Sir Alexander Fleming had washed his laboratory dishes. Fortunately, he made a mistake and left a mess over the weekend. Upon his return he found a hairy green substance growing in the dirty dishes. That was disturbing, but what caught his attention (a difference that made a difference) was that where the mold grew, bacteria did not. Naturally, prior training was necessary for him to be able to tell the difference between mold and bacteria, and also to perceive the lack of bacterial growth as significant. Normal Learning is important. However, it was the *mess* that catapulted Fleming from "more of the same old stuff" into genuine innovation.

Over the years I have collected anecdotal evidence from clients and colleagues concerning the circumstances surrounding real breakthroughs. The interesting thing is that absolutely none of them ever occurred according to plan. While I may have found only what I was looking for (which is usually the case), I am still searching for a breakthrough that happened the way it was supposed to. This search began while I was at the National Institutes of Health (Heart, Lung, and Blood Institute). While there I had the privilege of meeting a number of very senior researchers, including a few Nobel Laureates. My question was always the same: Did they know of any major breakthrough, including their own, which happened according to "the plan"? Nobody seemed to. I have continued this search in areas other than biomedical research, with no positive results to date.

The Birth of Fiberglass: Making Opportunity Out of a Mess

Fiberglass, the discovery and major product of Owens/Corning Fiberglas (OCF), began with a mess. Shortly before World War II, OCF was seriously looking for other ways of using what it knew best, glass-making technology. Up to that point it had largely been making bottles, but with the advent of plastic, it looked as if the bottle market might take a dive. So the search began for new applications and products.

One fine day, their director of research decided that if a way could be found to weld glass blocks (the sort you build transparent walls with), that would be a new, marketable product. I have never been clear exactly why he thought this was so, but he did. In any event, he summoned his research assistant, one Dale Kleist, and directed him to figure out the appropriate means.

Dale obediently assembled a pile of glass blocks, a gas torch, and glass rods, and set about doing what he had been told. Unfortunately the fruits of his labor were not as envisioned. The harder he tried, the messier things got. As he melted the glass rods with the gas torch, preparatory to "welding," the force of the escaping gas blew the molten glass all over the floor—in long thin fibers. In a very short time, he had accumulated a considerable pile, and so far as he was concerned, the grand experiment was a disastrous mess.

As Kleist was reaching despair, the director returned to the scene of the crime. Kleist was prepared for the worst, but instead of loudly denouncing him for failure, the director was enraptured. What he saw in that mess was the tensile quality of the glass fibers, and fiberglass was born.

The curious thing about this story is that forty years later, when I was consulting with a division of the company, virtually nobody remembered it, except for a few old-timers. That moment in OCF history displayed some useful examples of how to make an opportunity out of a mess.

The situation at OCF was a common one in the 1980s. The corporation had been attacked by a corporate raider, and management was doing its best to hold on. In the final round, management won, but it was a bittersweet victory. In order to meet the ransom the company sold businesses and closed facilities, to the point that once-robust annual sales of $4 billion shrank to a little more than $2 billion.

Even more critical was the fact that, even though not everybody lost their jobs (many folks went with the sold businesses), there was a very significant reduction in the workforce. This meant that the business that remained had to be done with many fewer hands. It is a testimony to those who stayed that they put their best foot forward and rallied the company, but at tremendous cost. Fourteen-hour days, seven days a week, and at the end of six months, these folks were simply exhausted. There comes a point when you can't run any faster; you have to run smarter. But the options for smart running seemed limited indeed. It was a simple case of playing a new ballgame by rules created in the halcyon days when money and staff were no problem.

And they had forgotten their story. Once upon a time, OCF had made opportunity out of a mess, virtue out of a mistake, new business out of a failed experiment. And doing all that again would be infinitely easier if they could remember having done it once before. No guarantees, of course.

How could they forget their story? The question really bothered me, and I have no certain answer, but I did notice a curious coincidence. Shortly before the fall, OCF was proudly investing an incredible amount of money to support research. Millions of dollars went to maintaining a large research campus, with 1,200 employees. Everything was carefully managed. Programs and systems were piled on top of each other, all dedicated to ensuring the relevance of research to market needs. It was a well-oiled machine with no chaos allowed. There was, however, one small problem. According to local lore, the preceding 10 years of carefully managed research had produced absolutely no new products. Safer products, prettier products. But nothing new.

Given their recent history, it would have been very difficult to admit that everything had begun with a mess. And as a matter of fact, it is quite unlikely that given the way they were doing research, fiberglass would ever have been discovered. Rather, that mass of messy glass fibers would have been swept up, and Dale Kleist directed to take some new approach. After all, you have to stick with the plan. As for the story of Dale Kleist? Better forget the whole thing.

Breakthrough Technology

A research department of DuPont retained my services to assist them in achieving what they called "Breakthrough Technology." Apparently they saw the market taking some interesting, and not necessarily beneficial turns, and thought they should get ahead of the game. In the course of this assignment, I met with the directors of the several local laboratories, and asked them whether they had ever had any breakthroughs, on the grounds that if it had ever happened before, we would at least know what we were looking for.

After some thought, they identified six events that qualified. To this day, I am not entirely sure what they actually were, as each seemed to involve stranger ways of twisting molecules, none of which I understood. But the directors were satisfied, and that was all that counted.

In order to get some sense of the importance of these breakthroughs, I asked what would be the profitability of their product line had these breakthroughs *not* occurred, and all agreed that the current bottom line results would not be pleasing.

My next question was a little rougher. How many of these breakthroughs, I asked, occurred according to plan, with the right people doing the right thing at the appropriate time and place, all within budget? There was a very long pause. And the answer, when it came, seemed more than a little embarrassing. None.

Then I went to the heart of the matter, and asked whether any of them had almost failed, not for technical reasons, but for other causes. There was an even longer pause, and eventually two candidates were named, but the reasons remained unstated. I asked why, and a young manager answered almost sheepishly, "When we tried to manage them."

It struck me as both strange and sad that the only successes that these folks could identify occurred in spite of their best efforts to do what they were supposed to do: manage. Further, failure loomed when they did their job.

Eventually the silence was broken by the same young manager who had last answered my question. He said, "Harrison, I think we are wasting a lot of our money and your time. All we have to do is do intentionally what it seems we are doing anyhow." I couldn't disagree with him, and that session marked the end of my assignment.

The simple truth of the matter was that these laboratory directors held a notion of research and innovation so predicated on orderly, programmed activity, that they simply couldn't recognize (without prodding) any significant event (read "breakthrough") which occurred outside of their expectations. Obviously they all "knew" that the break-throughs had occurred, but their occurrence was treated as an aberrant phenomenon, an exception to the rule of ordered research. It turned out, of course, that the exception was the rule.

There is nothing approaching proof here, but in 30 years of asking I have never found any person, presumably involved in innovative activities, who could remember any time that the breakthrough occurred according to plan. That may be faulty memory on their part, or faulty listening on mine. But that is the situation, and I believe it is significant.

CHAOS, INSPIRATION, AND SPIRIT

In the presence of breakthrough moments, when High Learning is running at top speed, it is very easy, and probably inevitable, that we should fixate on the concrete results. Penicillin is born, fiberglass invented.

But if we look closer, we are sure to discover something deeper. Call it inspiration-at-work. No matter what the details, we can feel, if not see, the power of the human Spirit breaking boundaries and discovering new ways of being in the world, doing things, getting on with life. It is not always pretty, but it is definitely exciting. It seems that inspiration comes in strange packages with the terrifying label, *Some Assembly Required.*

Once the breakthrough moment has passed, the mess must be cleaned up and ordered processes developed to utilize the new discovery. But the moment itself is special, we might say inspiring, which literally means *in-spirited.* With the presence of chaos, space is opened, and Spirit always seems to show up.

If we miss the presence of Spirit in the white-hot moments of discovery, the presence of Spirit is inescapable in those scary times of organizational meltdown. It may not be a happy Spirit, but there is no question that in those times that truly try our souls, we get right down to basics. Who are we, what are we doing here, and where do we go anyhow?

As the climax approached in the saga of Owens/Corning Fiberglas, senior executives found themselves in a maelstrom of activity. The only certainty was that nothing was certain, and they had to find some new way of doing business that would be acceptable to the banks, stockholders, customers, and employees. The name of the game was reorganization, not once, but dozens of times. Not that each organizational plan was implemented, but many were laid on the table as appropriate fit and function were sought. In the words of the chaos theorists, it was Periodic Doubling with a vengeance, and total chaos was just around the corner.

In the midst of it all, there were periods of momentary respite, even silence, when it became possible, even mandatory, to ask the painful questions: Why bother? What does it all mean? Asking such questions runs the risk of coming up with a troubling answer: there is no reason. And that can sometimes be beneficial.

On the other hand, the posing of the questions can also create deeper opportunities. In the case of at least one OCF executive, I believe that occurred. After most of the dust had settled, this executive reflected on the situation as follows:

We re-reorganized so many times that more than occasionally, I couldn't remember who we were. But the remarkable thing is that through it all we never lost our Spirit. However, if we had lost that, I think we would have lost it all.

The true Spirit of an organization often gets buried in the daily round of important things to be done. For a period of time that situation is of no consequence, for after all, the business is being accomplished. But there comes a time when the state of the Spirit becomes of more than incidental concern.

The initial signs are usually quite small and very forgettable. People just don't seem as involved and excited as they were in the "old days." At first, such observations are passed off as the nostalgic remembrances of the old-timers. But then it seems that something deeper may be involved. Organizational relationships become frayed, tempers snap. Arguments and backbiting break out for no apparent reason. The "zinger" replaces genuine humor in corporate conversation. And the great "They" emerges as the source of all evil. They did this, They didn't do that, but nobody ever saw "They."

Eventually more serious signs of a sagging Spirit surface. Vision goes, innovation slows, and creativity is visible mostly by its absence. Customers go unheard, and quality is only something to talk about. A sagging Spirit is a weak Spirit, which inevitably produces a sagging bottom line. For the truth of the matter is, Spirit is the bottom line.

Coming to this realization, or remembering it, is never a pleasant experience, for it usually occurs in the midst of chaos. At precisely the moment when we need every ounce of spirited participation that we can muster, the Spirit has apparently gone on vacation and off the job. That should come as no surprise, for nobody was taking care of the Spirit. Somehow, it just didn't seem to be an important thing to do.

chapter 3

Chaos, Order, and the Creative Process

In the first blush of excitement generated by the appearance of chaos theory, there was a fixation on chaos. Blame it on the media if you like, because chaos was news, and order was not. *Chaos theory*, however, is actually a misnomer, for the news was not so much about chaos, but rather the apparent contradiction that chaos has an order, or perhaps better said, order emerges in the midst of chaos.

Truth to tell, the real excitement was neither chaos nor order, but rather what happens in between, which we might call creation. Somehow, in the great dance taking place between chaos and order, something new emerges. That "new thing" could be a living cell, a small creature, you, your friends, or a combination of any or all of the above, which we might call an *organization*, or in contemporary jargon, a system.

Organizations or systems come in all shapes and sizes. In the human sphere we have families, businesses, and countries, just to name a few. Beyond us, we discover ecosystems, planetary systems, and ultimately the cosmos itself. As vastly different in appearance and size as these systems may be, they share common bonds: at some point in time they came into existence, over time they change, and some time they end. In short, they have a life.

For reasons that need not concern us at the moment, we seemingly become infatuated with how any system is at a particular point in time. It becomes, in our mind, a discrete *thing*, which may appear permanent or even immortal. If this *thing* happens to be your family, business, or country, such attribution of changelessness is quite understandable. After all, it gives us a sense of security. The *thing* will be the same over time, and we have a sense of equilibrium, a sense of balance.

As understandable as our infatuation with equilibrium may be, there is a cost. We fail to heed the admonition of Arnold Mandell, who reminded us that, "When you reach an equilibrium in biology, you are dead." And all the things we really care about have a life—families, businesses, countries—which we hope will continue.

It may occur to us that perhaps we are looking at the wrong thing. Indeed, we should not be looking at any *thing* at all, but rather at the *process* by which the thing (whatever it may be) has come into existence and continues on its merry way toward whatever destiny. When we turn our eyes from the thing itself, the physical form of a particular organization for example, to the process of life, there appears to be a pattern. In classical religious terms this pattern is usually described as life, death, and resurrection. If we wish to avoid the religious connotations of these terms, the same thing can be said in the language of the chaos theorists: Steady State, Periodic Doubling, chaos, and reconstitution at a new and higher level of complexity. Of course there is also the possibility that the system will crash and burn.

The process as described is linear, which is true. But it is also infinitely more complex than the three to four steps mentioned above. At any given time, in any given system, any or all of the stages described may be taking place. Even though it seems like business as usual (Steady State), somewhere in the bowels of the organization chaos is breaking out, Periodic Doubling lurches on its way, and it may even be that new organization is becoming manifest. It is all in a day's work. Of course there are times when the whole system goes into chaos, but even there, as our chaos theory friends remind us, there is a pattern and the possibility of emergent order.

All of this is terribly confusing to those who have been educated to expect precise, defined, well-ordered stages and steps. In truth, descriptions that look fine on paper don't turn out quite the same way in life.

THE LIMITATIONS OF LANGUAGE
AND THE USE OF DIALECTIC

Here we run into some of the hard facts of language. Pick any word you want, and it never quite captures what you have in mind. Words (or their mathematical equivalents), however, are the building blocks of thought, or certainly the means by which we communicate thoughts. We thus face the curious possibility that to say something completely is to say nothing at all.

There is, however, another way of dealing with the paradox of language without instantaneously throwing up our hands in despair at what seems to be an outright contradiction. That way is well known in philosophy and theology, but hardly commonplace in the world of business and organizations. That way travels under several names, including *polarity* or *dialectic*. If you can't say exactly what you want with a single word, try two, but understand that neither word by itself will do the job. In everyday situations we use this technique when trying to describe the color of something, as in "It's sort of blue-grey." It is neither blue nor grey, but something in the middle.

The technicalities of this approach need not be dealt with at the moment, but surely the general idea is clear. The meaning we want to communicate shows up in the tension (polarity, dialectic) between the two words we have used. We don't care about "blueness" or "greyness" but something in the middle.

For those of us in the West, who have grown up with the notion that truth is in the facts, and facts have to be identified with exacting precision such as with one word or a single number, all of the above appears as sloppy thinking. Yet most of the rest of the world has been quite content to allow meaning to appear in the middle.

This is not to suggest that striving for precision is a bad thing, as long as this striving is tempered with the realization that there are some things we can't quite say, exactly. At best our words and our numbers, even when carefully defined and used, create only maps of the territory we explore. To confuse the map with the territory, as Alfred Korzybski[1] reminds us, is to invite disaster.

CHAOS, ORDER, AND THE CREATIVE PROCESS

With this short excursus on the limitations of language behind us, we may now return to the central concern: chaos, order, and the creative process. I suggest that our fundamental concern is neither chaos nor order, but rather what happens in between—in the tension, polarity, or dialectic established by the two.

At the risk of mind-bending sophistry, I believe it to be true that in the natural world neither chaos nor order exist in pure states. Pure chaos, if such were to exist, would be absolute nothingness—no meaning, no pattern, no nothing. Pure order, if such were to exist, wouldn't be much better—total homogenized sameness, nothing moving, nothing going anywhere.

Everything we know is on a journey from one state to another: out of chaos into order, out of order into chaos. Never resting. Even apparently inert rocks are on such a journey, albeit a slow one. After all, as high-energy physicists would remind us, once you get below the surface it is all energy, possibly stable for the moment, but just waiting for an excuse to break loose.

We have now returned to our starting point at the beginning of the chapter. On the table we have chaos, order, and the creative process. Our central concern is the creative process itself, and the way in which that process apparently works itself out in the middle of chaos and order. Hopefully it is now clear that the creative process is to be identified with neither chaos nor order, and to choose one as "good" and the other as "bad" is to miss the point. Neither one, by itself, leads to creation.

It is the dance *between* chaos and order that is truly creative. Sometimes this dance is characterized primarily by chaotic destruction, as ground is cleared and space opened for the new order to appear. At other times the given order appears unchanging, but the wise will know that at some moment the world will change again, and the new order will be the old order. The dance will continue. At least that is the story, and it is a story we (all of us) have been telling for a very long time.

Ancient Versions of the Tale

As we have previously noted, virtually all of the ancient traditions of humankind, at least the ones I know about, are agreed that chaos is no stranger, that order is not the end of the game, and that the process of creation takes place between the two. Thus Shiva dances as Destroyer and Creator, the Tao emerges between the yin and the yang, and Yahweh (the God of Israel) brings forth a people and a world through peace and destruction. For obvious reasons, we may prefer order, but we *need* chaos to plow the fields of existence so that the seeds of new life may germinate and grow.

There is another word for the creative process, particularly as it works out in the human arena: *transformation*. Traditionally, transformation refers to the passage of the human Spirit (consciousness) through various formal manifestations, or states, on the way to whatever fulfillment may be in store. Transforming, as it were. That is the old story, which remains powerful for many of us. But there is a newer story, which may be more appealing to those of us who have found the ancient religious traditions to be less than useful in the modern world.

Complex Adaptive Systems: Self-Organization in Molecular Systems

"Complex Adaptive Systems" is the signature designation for self-organizing systems created by the people at the Santa Fe Institute. Way down there in New Mexico, this illustrious group of scientists have been thinking and working on the issue of self-organizing systems for many years. While not alone in this endeavor, I think few would argue with their being placed on the very short list of major contributors to our growing knowledge of the field.

The work of Stuart Kauffman, a theoretical biologist and sometime member of the institute, has special relevance to our discussions. Kauffman set himself the awesome task of discovering how it is that we (all of us) managed the journey from primal ooze to you, or me, or all living creatures. How could it be that a mulling broth of stuff, in a relatively short time (geologically), passed from disassociated molecules to organic beings? Traditionally, of course, most humans would answer, "God did it." That may well be right, but if you are not sure there is a God, and/or you are still curious about how it all came to be, Kauffman's question (quest) is a critical one.

Many years of research, in the laboratory and with computer modeling, have brought Kauffman to the position that given a small number of essential preconditions, it just happened. Or as he says with almost mantra-like regularity, "Order for Free!"

Not all of Kauffman's colleagues will agree with his conclusions in detail, and doubtless there are some who feel he has totally gone off the deep end, but if footnotes in a variety of scholarly publications are any indication of acceptance, Kauffman has made his mark, if not with the specifics, then certainly at the level of generalization.

The essential preconditions for self-organization, according to Kauffman, are the following:

1. A nutrient-rich, relatively protected environment
2. A high level of diversity and potential complexity in terms of the elements present
3. A drive for improvement
4. Sparse pre-existing connections between the various elements
5. It is all (the whole mess) at the edge of chaos

I should note that nowhere does Kauffman outline the necessary preconditions precisely as I have, but I believe I have caught the essence.

Nutrient-Rich, Relatively Protected Environment For the process of self-organization to begin, a relatively safe environment must exist. You don't want it too safe or condition #5 (edge of chaos) will be violated, but some protection from the destructive gales of the surrounding world is required. In terms of our early history this might mean that the surface of the earth had cooled sufficiently that new collections of atoms and molecules were not instantly fried.

Diversity/Complexity The likelihood of self-organization is increased when there are all sorts of different things floating about. Some of these "things" may actually end up as part of the final package. Other elements may simply assist the process as catalysts. The analogy is possibly inappropriate, but I like to think of a good party. If everybody there is exactly the same, all middle management from the same organization for example, the party never seems to get off the ground. In fact it is dreadfully dull.

However, if there is a broad mix of folks, interesting things start happening. Some of the people form little clusters where wonderful new ideas are generated. Other folks never seem to join these groups, but make the necessary introductions so that strangers may find their commonality. Catalysts as it were.

A Drive for Improvement These are my words, and not Kauffman's, but the idea is that somewhere resident in the whole mess is the "desire" to become a better mess. I have placed quotes around *desire* because I am not at all sure that you can, or should, talk about atoms having intentionality. But something of the sort seems to take place. In evolutionary theory, this is the concept of *fitness*. A driving force in the evolutionary process of anything—human, beast, or molecule—is the need to *fit* with the environment. Those who fit better, do better, and consequently survive and thrive. Change the environment, even a little bit, and the process starts once again. If you are a brown bear and the environment turns to ice and snow, you tend to stand out like a skunk at a garden party. Hunting becomes all but impossible when your prey can see you coming for miles. You just don't fit in. But change that brown to white, and presto-chango—the polar bear.

Sparse Connections The notion here may be a little difficult to grasp, but the analogy with a good party may help. If all who come are old friends and colleagues, with long-standing and well-worked-out associations, the party may be very comfortable (not necessarily bad), but generally not what you would call innovative and exciting. In essence it is all hardwired. What you see is what you get, indeed what you have had for a long time. Self-organization under these circumstances is hardly possible. It is already organized. Change the scenario by adding a lot of new folks, and things can get interesting indeed. It's not necessarily comfortable, but something new is going on.

At the molecular level, according to Kauffman, something rather similar seems to happen. When the molecular stew is composed of a diversity of elements with few prior connections, atoms tend to get together to form molecules, and simple molecules do the same and produce complex molecules. Kauffman even can throw some numbers at this phenomenon. If there are more than two connections between any element and the rest of the stew, self-organization doesn't seem to happen, or if it does, then very slowly. Absent those connections, and things really come together.

Edge of Chaos Here's the kicker: nothing much happens unless the whole mess is on the edge of chaos. Not pure chaos, mind you, but flirting with catastrophe. This is Kauffman's way of saying that chaos is essential for the evolutionary process. If the whole thing sits like a lump, the ongoing journey comes to a halt. Stated bluntly like this, it all seems quite obvious: no chaos, no evolution. But the obvious often escapes us. Doubtless it is our propensity for security that drives us to label chaos as "bad" and somehow antithetical to all that we hold good, true, and beautiful in life. But if Kauffman is right, and my experience makes me a believer, without chaos there is no life. After all, *"when you reach an equilibrium in biology, you are dead."*

Complex Adaptive Systems: Definitions

When the preconditions are right, the result is a Complex Adaptive System. No fuss, no bother—it just happens.

So just what is a Complex Adaptive System? Pretty much what the words imply. It is *complex* in that it has multiple elements, each representing a complexity in themselves, but further complexified by virtue of the myriad interrelationships manifest in their working together. It is complexity twice confounded.

The system is *adaptive* in that it is constantly seeking better ways to fit with its environment. This may be a matter of developing longer legs to facilitate catching dinner, or sharper, perhaps specialized teeth with which to eat that dinner. As the environment changes, so does the system, lest it be marginalized, or simply disappear.

Hidden within the word *adaptive* are some exciting possibilities, which we might explore at greater length down the road, but for the moment, we'll take just a taste. Adaptation, at least as used by Kauffman and others, is but another way of talking about learning. Complex Adaptive Systems *learn*, and learning appears as a natural and automatic aspect of their being. It would appear then that in the world of self-organizing systems not only is "order for free," but *learning is for free*. It just happens as a natural consequence of the systems being in the world. Considering all the interest and effort devoted to the creation of learning organizations, it may turn out that our systems (Complex Adaptive Systems) are just *naturally* Learning Organizations. You don't have to do a thing.

The folks in Santa Fe, and Kauffman in particular, make a very convincing case for the existence and function of self-organizing systems, by whatever name. But (and it is a very large *but*) most of their work relates to molecular stew on the way to becoming various creatures. How do we know that their findings also apply to human systems, such things as businesses, government agencies, and the local pizza parlor? And what would it mean anyhow? A partial answer to these questions seems to be coming from better than a decade and a half's experience in Open Space.

THE OPEN SPACE EXPERIMENT: SELF-ORGANIZATION IN HUMAN SYSTEMS

In 1985, Open Space Technology was born. It emerged not so much as a product of intentional design, but rather as an outgrowth of frustration and at some level, laziness. The frustration appeared as a result of my having spent an entire year organizing an international gathering for 250 people, only to discover that the best part, as judged by all participants and myself, were the coffee breaks. It was during the coffee breaks where the real juicy stuff happened. All the rest (featured speakers, panel discussions, and the like) seemed almost like an interruption to the core activity. It is pretty hard to take when you are forced to recognize that one year's hard work basically yielded a continuing sequence of interruptions to the main activity. There had to be a better (and simpler) way.

Inspiration for Open Space came from a small village in West Africa called Balamah, where I was privileged to be a guest of the chief for a period of time. I noticed that everything of importance happened in a circle. The elders met in a circle, the village danced in a circle. The men held council in a circle, and the women gathered for their tasks and conversations in a circle. It seemed that there must be some magic in a circle. My thought at the time was that we could invite participants in a meeting to sit in a circle, add some simple mechanism to allow topics of interest to surface (a bulletin board would do), and provide an equally simple mechanism to determine the time and place of meeting in order to deal with the issues raised (a marketplace). It would then be entirely possible to share the magic of the Balamah circle with a much broader audience.

In the intervening years, I believe my hunch has proven correct. To date, thousands of groups ranging in size from 5 to 1,500 have gathered on virtually every continent to deal with an almost unimaginable diversity of topics. They have all begun in a circle, and each group has discovered what the people of Balamah have known forever. There is power in the circle, to the point that within a very short time (typically 15 minutes) a group is enabled to move from chaotic disparity to focused and productive activity.

PASSION AND RESPONSIBILITY

The circle is enlivened by two critical elements: passion and responsibility. People come to the circle because they care, in many cases very passionately, about the subject at hand, which could be anything—the future of their country, the renewal of their organization, or something as concrete as the enhancement of the manufacturing process of doors on airplanes. If they don't care, they don't come. More to the point, if they don't care, they *shouldn't* come. Not everybody cares about the same things, and having uncaring people in an Open Space circle, is, to put it bluntly, a drag. They contribute nothing, and they gain nothing.

To ensure that people really do care, *voluntary self-selection* is essential. At this point, Open Space differs hugely from the standard practice of requiring attendance on the seemingly sensible grounds that if everybody did just what they wanted to, nothing useful would get done. And yet, don't we all know that good work is rarely performed by people who don't care to do it? Contrary to the conventional wisdom, the Open Space experience has demonstrated time and again that given people who care, good things happen. Forcing people to do that which they really don't want to do is a bummer.

The second critical element in Open Space is responsibility. Nothing gets done until, or unless, people take responsibility for doing it, and responsibility is a direct function of caring. Thus at the beginning of an Open Space, those present are invited to identify any issue or opportunity related to the central concern (the future of their company, for example) for which they have real passion and are willing to take responsibility by placing that issue on the table for discussion and resolution. Contrary to what might be expected, this really works.

THE PRINCIPLES AND THE LAW OF OPEN SPACE

Over time we have identified four principles and one law to assist participants in the navigation of Open Space. In fact, both the principles and the law are less instructions for what should be done than an acknowl-edgment of what happens anyhow. The four principles are:

1. Whoever comes are the right people.
2. Whatever happens is the only thing that could have.
3. Whenever it starts is the right time.
4. When it is over, it is over,

The first principle reminds people not to be worried about folks who are not there, but to concentrate on those present, knowing that they are there because they care, and that caring automatically makes them the right people. Others might have come, possibly should have come, but they did not care enough to come.

The second principle, *Whatever happens is the only thing that could have*, is a blatant statement of the obvious. There is no point worrying about what could have been, should have been, might have been. What is, is the only thing at the moment. And that is all we can deal with right now.

The third principle, *Whenever it starts is the right time*, is anathema to most Western managers, but the rest of the world understands this is just the way things are. Actually, the principle is all about Spirit, or more exactly inspired performance, which does not start when the clock says so, but only when it is ready.

The final principle, *When it is over, it is over*, reminds people, in Open Space and elsewhere in life, that all things come to an end, even though you cannot tell when that end will come. At such a time, it is over, and it is time to let go and move on.

The one law, which we call *The Law of Two Feet*, goes as follows: If at any time you find yourself in any situation where you are neither learning nor contributing, use your two feet. This may appear rude and disruptive, but it says no more than what we would do anyhow, although instead of using our two physical feet, we find our minds and hearts wandering to faraway places. In Open Space it is much better to follow your heart than to sit still feeling miserable, and probably mak-ing everybody else miserable as well.

Open Space can be done in a variety of time frames, but for truly important and complex issues, 2½ days is just about right. With that amount of time, the following outcomes are virtually guaranteed:

1. Every single issue of concern to anybody present will be on the table, if they choose to put it there.
2. All issues will receive full discussion.
3. A full written report of all discussions and conclusions will be in the hands of all participants upon departure.
4. All issues will be ranked in priority order.
5. Top "Hot" issues will be identified.
6. Issues related to the Hot issues will be clustered.
7. Immediate, next step actions will be developed and responsibility assumed.

ACCOMPLISHMENTS IN OPEN SPACE

Perhaps more remarkable than the substantive outcomes of an Open Space gathering are the manifest behaviors evidenced by the groups involved, in addition to the general "feel" of the gathering. Such things as self-managed work groups, distributed and abundant leadership, personal empowerment, appreciation of diversity—to name a few—are the apparently automatic results of Opening Space. Special training to achieve these results is not required, and indeed magic words such as "self-managed work groups" are never uttered. All of the above just seems to happen.

Substantive accomplishments in Open Space are as various as the bodies of people who have used the approach. But in all cases in my experience the results have been viewed with an odd mixture of disbelief and awe. Disbelief that so much could be done, and awe at the power of the human Spirit that did the job. Some even call it magic.[2]

A case in point involved an AT&T design team, which did in two days what it had anticipated might take ten months and a $200 million budget. The story is an all-too-familiar one. The group had been assigned the responsibility for the design of the AT&T Olympic Pavilion, which they accomplished, and it took ten months. Then plans changed, but in a good way. The Olympic Committee invited AT&T to move its pavilion from the edge of the Global Village to dead center, and since the corporation was investing primarily in one thing, called exposure, this was an offer they could not refuse. But there was a problem. At the edge, they could anticipate 5,000 visitors a day. In the center the number could leap to 75,000. In short, the old design was dead; and worse, only seven months remained before the start of the games, in which the pavilion must not only be designed but built.

Twenty-three rather unhappy people met in a circle facing each other and a task they believed to be virtually impossible in the time available. But there was a happy ending. Forty-eight hours from start, the group had created a totally new design, down to the level of rough working drawings. They all agreed the new design was aesthetically better than the first one, and they were actually farther along with its implementation, because as they were designing, they simultaneously ordered up the necessary supplies and material. Perhaps most important, they were still talking to each other, and the only complaint was that they had not used Open Space in the first place. The AT&T executive responsible called it magic.

As of the present moment, I can't think of a single type of group that has failed to thrive in an Open Space environment. Students, teachers, executives, folks on the shop floor, sugar cane workers, Native Americans, African tribesmen, politicians, federal bureaucrats, and even lawyers—all seem to do very well.

Perhaps we will find some group somewhere that does not follow what seems to be the norm, but to date such a group has not appeared, so far as I know. Regardless of size, ethnicity, political persuasion, sex, age, economics, education, national origin, professional position, religion—Open Space seems to work just fine.

To be fair, however, we have found one circumstance where Open Space will not work and should never be tried. In those situations where attachment to specific, predetermined outcomes is paramount, Open

Space is a dismal flop, not because it doesn't work, but because it does. It seems that the people involved take the invitation of Open Space to heart, follow what they really care about, and become very creative. Under such circumstances, the predetermined outcomes largely go out the window.

Thus in the vast majority of situations, Open Space works, and works very well. The central questions are: Why? And where do we go from here?

THE "WHY" OF OPEN SPACE

For a number of years, when asked when Open Space was appropriate, my answer was that Open Space can be used in any important situation characterized by:

▼ High levels of complexity in terms of the issue
▼ High levels of diversity in terms of the participants
▼ High levels of potential or actual conflict
▼ When the "decision time" was yesterday

Do not use Open Space (as we noted above) when the issue is already settled and the outcome predetermined.

When I read Stuart Kauffman's work I realized that my conditions for use were not only factors that one need consider prior to embarking on an Open Space venture, they were in fact (presuming that Kauffman is correct) the essential preconditions for self-organization, albeit stated in slightly different ways. The "why" of Open Space, quite simply, is the phenomenon of self-organization. Open Space "works" because it is self-organization at work in the human domain.

Kauffman's Preconditions and Open Space

The preconditions for self-organization described by Stuart Kauffman have helped us understand the "why" of Open Space. Several of them (such as complexity and diversity) simply confirm what had already been observed, but some broke new ground, or helped us to see old things in deeper ways.

The *Search for Fitness*, which I have called a "drive for improvement," confirms the experience that Open Space simply doesn't work out very well when used in what might be called a "demonstration mode." Put somewhat differently, unless the participants are engaged in something they truly care about, and unless they are deeply invested in searching for productive solutions no matter what such solutions may be, the whole experience is pretty flaccid, and participants and onlookers typically will ask, "Is that all there is?"

The precondition called *Edge of Chaos* correlates with my observations about the necessary presence of potential or actual conflict. In Open Space, the presence of conflict on or beneath the surface indicates that the pot is sufficiently stirred and that something useful might happen. The issue is not to eliminate the conflict, but rather to provide sufficient space so that the energy locked in the conflicted parties may be turned loose to create new and more useful responses.

The phrase *Edge of Chaos* also conjures up an image that helps us understand Open Space at the level of theater, dance, or perhaps even psychodrama, for an actual Open Space event may be seen in any or all of these terms. At the beginning of an event, the participants are invited to sit in a circle, which means, of course, that there is an open space separating all of them. With larger groups (250 and up) there is a lot of open space. With the exception of a few pieces of paper and some magic markers, there is *nothing* in between. The reaction of the group to this space ranges from mild discomfort to something approaching awe, or even panic. People show a precise understanding of where the space begins. Like children facing a cold swimming pool, they will come to the edge, dip their toes, and back away. If they have to cross the space, they will typically scuttle across, spending as little time in the exposed environment as possible. For the most part people stand outside the circle of chairs, and only take their places at the last moment. Doubtless there are practical reasons for this behavior, but at a symbolic level (and I think symbol becomes reality here) that space is nothing short of something like the great cosmic void. It is pure chaos, or about as close as we can get. There is no meaning, no guidance, no structure telling people where to go and what to do. Just nothingness. If these perceptions have validity, then it is literally true that the group stands (or sits) at the edge of chaos.

The remaining precondition on Kauffman's list, *Sparsity of Connections,* requires that potential elements in the new, emergent order have as few prior connections as possible. Kauffman specifies two or less. I confess that the application of this precondition to the Open Space environment escaped me for a period of time, but upon reflection it became clear that deeply integrated groups (with tight structure and a long history) took marginally longer to self-organize than did groups more recently and loosely associated. The actual difference is usually a matter of minutes, if that, and therefore quite easily missed, but it was there.

With the connection established, I then found myself wondering about why tightly structured groups did as well as they did in Open Space. Kauffman's precondition would seem to suggest that such groups wouldn't have a chance, although the experience had been that except for a minimal slowness in their start-up, the actual performance of a group rooted in an ancient hierarchical institution was basically indistinguishable from that of any other group. I think the answer lies in the power of the circle and the presence of chaos in its midst.

The nature of a circle (of people) is that there is no clear front, back, top, or bottom, as contrasted with the more usual seating arrangement with rows of chairs and a dais. When people come to a circle, where they sit is a matter of choice, with virtually no structural guidance as to where they *should* sit. Hence the seating pattern tends to be random, depending more on time of arrival than on preexisting social structure. Rather like shuffling a deck of cards, preexisting patterns are disaggregated. The process of disaggregation is continued, and probably intensified by the presence (albeit symbolic) of chaos. In the nature of things, the members of the randomly disassociated group now equally face chaos—which seems to help complete the task of self-organization. All of this is pure surmise on my part, but it is a fact that social structure and history have little, if any, predictive power relative to the capacity of a group to function well in Open Space. All sorts of groups seem to do equally well.

From Open Space Event to Everyday Business

The Open Space experience provides a useful transition from the world of primeval ooze (the object of Kauffman's concern) to the rather different world of human organization. But Open Space is typically a one- to three-day event, which is greatly removed from the 365-day reality of everyday business. Is it possible that what we experience in an Open Space gathering may become a 365-day reality?

This needn't mean that each day starts out by sitting together in a circle and going through the formal "opening of space," although that might not be such a bad idea. Rather, I am thinking of the kind and quality of experience wherein new ideas and ways of working together just seemed to pop into existence. Leadership becomes a distributed function regardless of title or position. Those who had the passion and concern to see a project through to completion automatically become the leaders. And as projects change, so would the leadership. Personal empowerment and sense of self-worth appear in new ways every day.

At a practical level, one might expect prodigious leaps in productivity. Remember the AT&T design team doing in two days what they might have anticipated taking ten months for a $200 million project? Such an accomplishment would give new meaning to the words "competitive advantage" and there would be time left over for being with one's family, taking a vacation, or just hanging out. Convert the AT&T experience to a mathematical expression of productivity increase, and the numbers tend to blow the mind. We are looking at an increase of 150 times or 1500 percent. Since most folks would be well satisfied with a 15 percent increase, 1500 percent simply goes off the chart.

It all sounds almost too good to be true, and yet these, and much more, are the constant, common experiences in Open Space. So we know it can happen. The issue is, can it happen more, or even most, of the time? Phrased somewhat differently, the real question is: *Can we intentionally and consciously allow the power of self-organization to work for us?*

I believe the answer is affirmative. And in fact, I strongly suspect that we are actually much farther down the road in this direction than we might imagine, or maybe even hope for. But before we can take full advantage of the possibilities, we must somehow be convinced that self-organization in human systems is real. And that thought may take some getting used to, given our present experience and prior training. We all know, as only years of education and more years of living and working in organizations can teach, that truly productive organizations are carefully designed and tightly controlled. We all know that. But consider another viewpoint.

SELF-ORGANIZING HUMAN SYSTEMS—FOR REAL

Think of something really big and complicated, like the feeding of the population of the city of New York. Eight and a half million people with just as many different tastes and styles, all needing to be fed every day—usually three times. Now design a system that will accomplish what is needed. Pretty tough huh? But there is the point, there is no reason to do what has already been done. And truth to tell, nobody ever designed it. It just happened all by itself.

Obviously there are a few glitches here and there, but the system works, and it works quite well, as the residents and millions of tourists who frequent the city will attest. But please note, nobody designed it. Nobody is in charge. To be sure there are a few individuals and organizations who help out around the edges, such as the Health Department, the Restaurant Association, food critics in the several newspapers, along with assorted gurus and other pundits. But at the end of the day, day in and day out . . . the system does it all by itself.

Of course, you could substitute the name of any city or village in the world for New York, and the point would be the same, only stronger.

Self-organizing systems are naturally occurring phenomena in our world, only sometimes we are tempted to think that some individual or small groups actually did the deed.

Let me add one more example: the Internet. Bill Gates to the contrary, nobody controls the Internet, nor will they ever. To be sure, many have made a contribution, even as the myriad chefs of New York make their contribution, but in the final analysis, the Internet has a life of its own. You might think of it as the biggest Open Space gathering ever, or more importantly, a powerful example of self-organizing systems operating at the level of humankind.

Admittedly, these two examples are just teasers, but they are suggestive. Wouldn't it be wonderful if it were true? Before organizational theory, before systems design, before Scientific Management— self-organization was. And thank god, still is. It therefore remains only to acknowledge consciously what we have always been, and then carefully set about enjoying what we really are.

I find myself succumbing to an outrageous thought. *There is no such thing as a non-self-organizing system.* We, in all of our various manifestations (corporations, governments, social institutions, mom-and-pop stores), like all the rest of the natural order, are Complex Adaptive Systems. We need to learn to recognize this fact, and more importantly, to live and work in ways congruent with what we really are.

This new learning will not take place without some degree of pain and dislocation, but in most cases the pain will be to our egos. Up until now, some of us actually thought that we created and organized the systems in which we work. But should it turn out that natural systems, including human systems, are truly self-organizing, much of that effort was wasted. Pretty hard on the old ego, but useful for all of that. We might now learn to live with what will happen of its own accord, and build on that ordering in useful and appropriate ways.

part

Transformation
The Adaptive Process in Human Systems

HUMAN SYSTEMS, from families to the Family of Nations, share a common characteristic. They are all Complex Adaptive Systems. Like all other open, natural systems found anywhere in the cosmos, self-organization is simply what they do. It comes with the territory.

The claim that all human systems are self-organizing systems may well be unprovable, and if proof is a requirement for you, then I ask that you take the statement as a testable hypothesis, which it certainly is. For myself I feel quite comfortable with the assertion, at least sufficiently comfortable to explore what I perceive to be the more interesting questions: How does the process of adaptive self-organization take place in human systems, and are there some things that we might do to help it along?

I suggest that the self-organizing process in human systems is, at first glance, precisely the same as in all other systems. The simple preconditions for self-organization identified by Kauffman appear to correlate with what we have experienced in Open Space, our natural laboratory. Thus just as we, and all the rest of the created order, are bound by the laws of gravity, so also the elemental principles of self-organization apply clear across the board.

But there is a difference. If you drop a human being and a rock here on earth, both will fall in response to the law of gravity. The human being, however, will generally know that he or she is falling, and have some feelings about the matter. The rock, so far as we can tell, just falls.

The addition of *knowledge* and *feelings* (emotions) to the process of self-organization creates new dimensions in that process. Whereas the rock will simply get together with other rocks to create megarocks, we have some feelings about the matter, and maybe some choice.

The stakes for us are raised considerably by virtue of the traumatic nature of the adaptive process. An old order falters, dissolves, and (if fortune smiles) a new order emerges, more complex and better able to cope with the changing environment. If we were simply rocks, without knowledge and feelings, the process might be negotiated with equanimity. But we do have knowledge (awareness) of our past and present, and typically we have very strong feelings about both. Truthfully, we do not like losing what is old and familiar, and typically will resist such change to our dying breath, in some cases quite literally. Yet for the adaptive process to succeed we must let go of the old in order that the new may appear. Very painful. Very scary. How do we live through it?

chapter 4

The Standard Business Curve Revisited

WE HAVE ALWAYS KNOWN that things change, sometimes for better, and sometimes for worse. But we have hoped for the best, and generally speaking it has seemed that our various endeavors developed in a positive way.

In the world of business, this perception finds expression in the Standard Business Curve, a graphic seemingly emblazoned on the forehead of every MBA. Things start slowly, with a bare minimum of systems and products, followed by a take-off period when systems and products (to say nothing of plant, facilities, and employees) are added at something approaching an exponential rate. Finally, growth levels off, or proceeds upward at a gentle predictable rate, following a line that hopefully projects out to infinity, indicating the arrival of a mature business.

There is, however, one significant piece of data that never appears in the graphic representation of the Standard Business Curve. That datum, as Gregory Bateson points out, is common knowledge to every schoolboy. Somehow, however, it escaped the attention of the organizational theorists. Simply put: "What goes up will come down." It is never a question of "if," only "when." Sooner or later, the market will change, the product will become obsolete, the competition will intensify, the financial market will fall apart. Someday, somehow, somewhere, that rising business curve will come down, which necessitates a revision of the Standard Business Curve to reflect the truth of Bateson's dictum.

Every day we discover anew what every school-age child always knew: what goes up will come down.

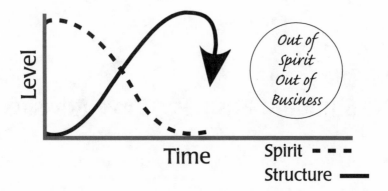

A NEW LINE ON THE CHART: THE SPIRIT LINE

While we are in the process of revising the trusty old Standard Business Curve, I propose a new line: the Spirit Line. This line suggests that the level of Spirit is inversely proportional to the level of structure. More directly: as structure goes up, Spirit goes down.

I am not sure that there is any way to prove this, but I believe it is the universal experience that all organizations start out in High Spirits. If it were not so, they probably would not have started at all. Everything is possibility, the slate is fresh. Excitement and innovation abound. That is the up side.

On the down side, there is another universal experience. Confusion also abounds. While innovation is always to be cherished, the truth is that it can be taken too far, especially when the wheel is reinvented for the umpteenth time. Sooner or later, somebody says the fateful words: *We have to get organized.* With that, structures, procedures, tables of organization, and all the rest, make their appearance.

Some of the original folks never get used to the new order, but most agree that getting organized is essential. There is, however, a price. Structure constricts the free flow of Spirit. That is by no means bad, for with structure and order come those qualities dear to the heart of every business person: efficiency, effectiveness, and profitability. Profit can rarely be returned when all available assets are devoted to reinventing the wheel.

For a time, and hopefully a long time, the benefits of efficiency, effectiveness, and profitability roll in. Unfortunately, however, as that time stretches out, people tend to forget that what drives it all is the Spirit of the place. Structure is only the highway upon which Spirit moves. Naturally, there is much useful work to be done keeping the highway in repair, adding improvements and controlling the traffic. This is called management, good management.

As long as the highway runs in some useful direction, and Spirit is content to travel that way, all well and good. But when the direction of good business changes, or Spirit tires of the same old view, difficulty emerges, and the end is at hand. What went up has just come down.

For those who never added the Spirit line to the Standard Business Curve, or who forgot the centrality of Spirit under the press of everyday affairs, the response at such a moment of ending is as understandable as it is futile. Frantic emergency actions are taken to shore up the structure and somehow get one more mile out of the old machine. Failing that (or in addition), Golden Parachutes break out for executives and job security contracts for employees. While these various strategies may work for a while, keeping people busy and hopefully feeling better, the truth of the matter is that when it is over, it is over. Ultimately, there is nothing to be done.

More accurately, there is nothing to be done with the structural side of things. There is plenty to be done with the Spirit.

RAISING SPIRIT:
A NEW STANDARD BUSINESS CURVE

If the model created by chaos/complexity theorists is disturbing, suggesting as it does that all Open Systems eventually go to chaos, it is also hopeful. At the other end of chaos, there is the possibility of a renewed existence, not along the same old lines, but actually an improved existence. There are no guarantees, of course, but if renewal is to occur in the organization, raising Spirit is a must. When the Spirit is up once more, it then becomes possible to generate new products, profits, and structure. So how do you raise Spirit?

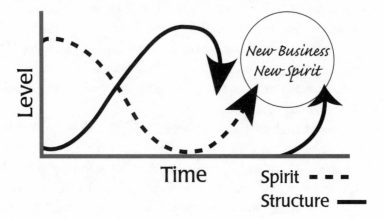

The subject of raising Spirit, if treated at all in the world of organizations, is usually handled under the heading of "motivation." In application, this turns out to be little more than the good old pep talk with some new bells and whistles, like recognition and rewards.

Pep talks are fine, but their utility diminishes when the team is not only losing, but virtually wiped off the field. As for recognitions and rewards, there is little to offer when bankruptcy, in one form or another, is the corporate reality. Pep talks under those circumstances do more harm than good. Everybody knows it is a charade, and it would be better to tell the truth and go home. There is a time for motivation, but not at the end. Something deeper is required.

The art and science of raising Spirit is not unknown. Indeed, humankind has been practicing it for all of recorded history, and undoubtedly before. It is called *Griefwork*. If this term is unfamiliar, the constituent words are not. It is quite simply the work of grief, or what grief does.

In most cases we experience grief as something that happens to us at those moments of ending, as opposed to a process that enables us to move from one state to a new one. This is quite understandable, for grief is intensely painful, and it is more than a little difficult to look beyond the pain of the moment to see the whole process.

A number of years ago, a small group of people, with Elisabeth Kübler-Ross[1] in the lead, looked beyond the pain of the moment in order to see the whole. And when they did, it was discovered that there was a process of grief that moved in recognizable stages, accomplishing predictable results.

You may be wondering how we got from the relatively benign subject of raising Spirit to a discussion of grief and death. The reason is quite simple. My experience has been that significant ending, in any area of life, produces the same reactions and results for those involved. Whether we are talking about the death of a loved one, or the death of a corporation, it is all death, and the reaction is identical.

To get the point, you need only remember those times in your own experience (or in the reported experience of others) when a plant closed, a business failed, or even some element of a business (a product line) was terminated. Listen to the conversation in the hallways, or at the locked plant gate in a one-industry town, and see if it doesn't sound a lot like a death in the family. And for good reason. When you have been doing a job for thirty years, and somebody tells you that it is over, you are losing more than a job. You are losing a way of life, and for some it is life itself. Time has been defined by the beginning and end of work. Hope has been articulated in terms of savings plans and bonuses. Progress has been measured by promotions and company recognition. And when that is gone, who are you, and what will you become? How do you tell your kids that the college education they expected can't be afforded? How do you explain to your spouse that the retirement home you dreamed of will never happen?

The reaction comes with deep, explosive anger and shock that such a thing could happen, and more acutely, happen to you. Then there is denial, the inability or unwillingness to acknowledge that anything has happened at all. Maybe it was just a bad dream that will vanish at the breaking of day.

Sound familiar? This is the normal, necessary, and productive process that each and every one of us goes through at significant moments of ending, when the Spirit is battered and hope is a four-letter word. This is grief working, or Griefwork. There is no way to eliminate the pain, but there are innumerable ways to shorten the time and improve the odds for a successful outcome—a renewed Spirit, ready to get on with the business of living. It all begins with knowing the process, and being willing and able to facilitate the journey.

There is another word to describe what is going on here: transformation, the process by which Spirit, or consciousness, passes through various manifest forms or states.

The process itself is not a pleasant one, for it involves letting go of a prior way of being, preparatory to the assumption of a new way of being. The problem is neither the old nor the new, but what is in between, which is often spoken of as *nothing* or the *void*. Nobody likes leaving the familiar, and we like even less hanging out in nothingness. But once on the other side, we experience ourselves in new and deeper ways, more capable of dealing with the world in which we find ourselves.

If the esoteric language of transformation is stripped to its essentials, it should sound very familiar to those who have engaged the thought of the chaos/complexity theorists as they have been working out the journey of complex adaptive systems and the process of self-organization. In traditional Christian terms, one might speak of life, death, and resurrection. Contemporary theorists would prefer Steady State, Periodic Doubling, chaos, and renewal at a higher order of complexity. Different words, same process—I think.

Contemporary theory relative to self-organizing systems is powerful, and in fact we might be able to look no further than its pronouncements in order to make sense out of our current situation, leaving to one side all discussions of transformation. But I think we would also lose a great deal, for what we experience in the evolving milieus of our organizations has as much, or more, to do with Spirit than simply biological or physical systems. By introducing the concept of transformation, we may link with the millennia-old experience of humankind as we have sought to understand ourselves in all of our dimensions—physical, biological, and spiritual.

chapter 5

Grief at Work

The Journey of Transformation

WHEN CHAOS STRIKES, transformation begins. The Spirit of a people enters a critical process with possible end results ranging from dissolution to the emergence of a radically new, more complex, adaptive organization. The process itself is that of grief working, enabling us to let go of what was in preparation for what is yet to be.

To some large extent, the process just happens all by itself. It cannot be avoided, nor can we change or skip the essential steps. Like the process of birth, there is a beginning, middle, and end. Nothing we can do will alter the natural progression. This, I believe, is self-organization at work, as the complex adaptive systems we are evolve to meet whatever destiny lies in wait.

Even though the process will happen pretty much by itself, there are ways to deepen the experience so that it is perceived as more than a cacophony of conflicting, painful happenings, but also as a creative enterprise in which we may participate and contribute. Knowing in advance the stages of this process may give us a sense of purpose and direction, even if such knowledge does nothing to eliminate the pain of passage. And with that knowledge comes the possibility of assisting ourselves and our fellows through the stages involved. Indeed there are some very concrete things that may be done as the process of transformation rolls along. But the role of the helper is exactly like the role of the midwife in birth. The midwife did not conceive the baby, will not bear the baby or raise it. But her presence can be extraordinarily helpful during the process. Our interests here are therefore both theoretical and practical. At the level of theory, I wish to offer a likely story descriptive of our transformational journey. Practically, I will point out certain things that can be done to speed the journey, possibly lessen the pain, and lead to the enhanced possibility of a positive outcome.

THE PROCESS DESCRIBED

Griefwork proceeds through definable and predictable stages. Each one is necessary and contributory to the end result. None can be skipped, even though we might wish there were a different way. In what follows we will track the process through:

- ▼ Shock and Anger
- ▼ Denial
- ▼ Memories
- ▼ Open Space as Despair
- ▼ Open Space as Silence
- ▼ Questioning
- ▼ Vision

and on to new organization.

Shock and Anger

Grief starts at the moment of ending or its imminent approach. The first phase is *shock and anger*. The actual expression varies with the language of the griever, but it is always some version of "Ohhh . . . shit!"

In effect it is purely a physiological response. Breathing in and breathing out. And there is a reason. With the insult of ending, people are likely to go into shock, and that often means stopping breathing. If you notice somebody in that condition, the shoulders are typically hunched forward. This is taken to be the posture of misery, which it is, but it is also very difficult to breathe, and without breath, life stops. So the first order of business is to get the patient breathing again, and shock and anger does the job.

This phase is quite noisy, and it is not uncommon for managers, and others who may be standing about at the time, to try and calm things down with direct orders or words of consolation. However, if we understand what is going on, that response is not only unhelpful, it is counterproductive. The point is to keep the patient breathing, and if saying "Oh shit!" does the job, so be it.

Sometimes a little encouragement is helpful. For example, I was working with a large American corporation in the midst of radical downsizing. People were losing jobs right and left, and those who escaped the axe felt almost as badly as those who did not, if only for reasons of guilt and also a certain knowledge that next time could be their turn. It was not a happy place, and the process of griefwork was off to a rocky start. People were simply sitting in shock, in stunned silence. There they were, sitting in neat rows, arms folded stoically across their chests, barely breathing. Radical action of some sort was clearly required.

I broke the silence with a question, "How are you feeling, folks?" More silence, indeed stony silence. Again I asked the question, "How are you feeling, folks?" And then way in the back corner of the room I heard a single voice say softly, "Oh shit."

That was my cue. I asked the gentleman for a repeat, and he obliged. I told the assembled group, "That's pretty good, how about more and louder?" Shortly we had a rousing "Oh shit" chorus echoing through the 23rd floor of the executive office building. I can't say the activity did much for corporate decorum, but I truly believe it saved the day for a number of those people. They were breathing again. And then they began to laugh as the ridiculous absurdity of the situation sank in. I knew a corner had been turned.

Shock and anger is emergency first aid. Administered quickly, life continues. But as a long-term strategy, it leaves a great deal to be desired. Some people, however, get stuck at this point, and spend the balance of their natural life in shock and deep anger. You find them in the back offices of companies that have gone through some transformative moment, and these folks never quite seem to get over it. At worst, they appear paranoid and their anger erupts at unpredictable and inappropriate times. Not exactly good for business.

The sad part is that this condition is largely preventable, for had the people been encouraged to fully express their shock and anger, when such expression was appropriate, those feelings would probably not have gone underground, only to reappear later.

Denial

The next phase of Griefwork is *Denial,* which often appears to be a terrible waste of time. In spite of all the evidence to the contrary, those involved persist in the obvious delusion that the end has not come. Were it a plant closing, the conversation would constantly turn to the notion that, "They aren't really going to close things down. It must be some kind of a trick just to get further contract concessions. After all, we've heard it before, and it never happened." The fact that it has now happened doesn't seem to register.

All exhortations to deal with reality fall on deaf ears. The people just can't hear. And they shouldn't. Not at that moment. Denial performs an essential function. Rather like the bandage on a wound, it provides protection so that healing can begin. When the pain of ending is so severe, it quite literally can't be dealt with, and denial offers anesthesia. Were it possible to crack through the denial and force the folks to acknowledge reality, it is quite likely the process not only would be retarded, but actually reversed. The folks would return to shock and anger.

Once again, the role of those who would care for Spirit is to provide the time, space, and permission for the process to take its ordered course. Any effort to move for early closure, or worse, skip a phase, will be entirely counter-productive.

As with shock and anger, people can also get stuck in denial. Such folks are not unknown in the corporate world, for never having acknowledged the ending of the old, they are incapable of dealing with the new, no matter how attractive that "new" may appear.

Memories

There will come a time when the reality of the situation finally can sink in, at which point the next phase, *Memories*, will begin. Superficially memories look and sound a lot like denial. But there is a difference, for now the fact of ending is acknowledged, if not totally accepted. All the memories of what happened, didn't happen, or might have happened, pass by.

The process is tedious to bystanders, for it appears that folks just keep talking about the same thing over, and over, and over again. Conversation focuses on the instant the bad news was delivered, and the question is, where were you at that dreadful moment. Everybody remembers in precise detail with endless repetition.

What sounds like boring repetition has a pattern and a purpose. The pattern is to start at the moment of ending, and work one's way backwards through all of the events leading up to the terminal moment. "I remember I was standing by my truck just waiting to go out on delivery, when Harry came running up with the news." Then silence.

Then again, "I was standing by the truck . . . Harry came running up . . . and you know minutes before I had just loaded in that marvelous new material my customers had been waiting for."

And again, "I was standing by the truck . . . Harry came running . . . marvelous new material . . . and you know, last week we had our most successful week ever . . . " So it goes, backwards.

What seems like pointless repetition is, in fact, accomplishing some very important work. There is a purpose. With each turn, the life history of those individuals, and that group, is effectively being rewritten to take into account the new reality. It is honoring the heroes, and the heroic events, so that they can be let go. Without that acknowledgment and honor, the tendency is to hang on to what was, not consciously perhaps, but hang on nonetheless. When getting on to the future is the issue, hanging on to the past is not helpful. In a curious way, one has to go backwards in order to make progress.

There is another valuable aspect to memories, which is to take inventory of current assets. Much of what is over, is over, but there will inevitably be certain things, called experience, that will serve well down the road. Reviewing this material is an essential precondition for placing it in order, ready for the next step.

For those concerned with caring for Spirit, the advent of memories offers an occasion to actually do something. Whereas the appropriate response to shock and anger followed by denial is to let it happen and listen, with memories some formal activities to speed the process can be initiated.

There are many names and forms possible here, and none are automatically "right," but the ancient institution of the Irish wake may be prototypical. For those who have never experienced such a thing, a short description will be in order.

Sometime after the departure of a dear brother, the clan assembles at the neighborhood pub. All through the night and on into the wee hours, glasses are raised and tales are told. The Dear Departed is celebrated in song and story, the good parts and the bad. When it is all over, usually with the rising of the sun, the heads may be hurting, but somehow the Spirit is refreshed. It is a new day and time to get on with life.

On occasion, I have actually held wakes for corporations and other organizations. I didn't use that term, but the intent and the effect were the same. As it turns out, you don't have to be Irish to reap the benefit.

Open Space as Despair

When the memories are over, a very solemn moment is reached: *Open Space*. Open Space is quite literally what the name implies, nothingness. It is all over.

My use of the words "Open Space" here may be confusing in the light of the prior discussion of Open Space Technology. Truthfully, the notion of open space as the center of the griefwork process occurred to me well before Open Space Technology ever happened. Open Space in the context of griefwork and transformation is closely akin to what the Buddhists might call the Void or Emptiness, or in Tibetan Buddhism, the Bardo, which is that "space" one crosses from this existence to the next.[1] Open Space Technology was so named because it appeared to me that the experience was similar to, or even the same as those deepest moments of passage.

The Open Space of our lives is experienced initially as Despair (without hope), because there is nothing left to hope *in*. All of the structures, procedures, and relationships that used to give life meaning are gone. There is nothing to count on, which means there is nothing to pin your hopes on. The pain of despair is intense, but it is also cathartic, carrying out the last remnants of what was. It is the final "letting go."

For some, the pain of despair can be so intense, and the fear of loss so profound, that the last moment of letting go never fully arrives. For them the balance of their natural lives will be lived in despair. Having nothing to look forward to, and nothing to fall back on, they become caught in the awful middle ground of meaninglessness. In the world of work, such people can be seen filling their days with trivia. Punching the time clock is all that matters.

Others, probably the majority of us, somehow use the moment of despair in a positive way. Rising above the pain, or maybe more accurately *embracing* the pain, the cathartic properties of despair are allowed to do their work. In a curious fashion, the way out of despair is not to avoid it, but to embrace it. The searing agony is replaced by a bittersweet sense of peace.

Open Space as Silence

With the arrival of the sense of peace comes *Silence*. Beyond shock and anger, denial, memories, and despair there is silence. There is no clock that can measure the duration of this moment, indeed it seems to be a moment totally out of time. Calling this a pregnant moment seems almost trivial, but very true. *Holy* seems more appropriate. This is the moment of creation. With everything gone, nothing remains to prevent the emergence of the new. It is all over. It is all potential. At this instant, if ever, differences can be perceived that truly can make a difference. The moment of silence is therefore also a learning moment of the profoundest sort, the time of High Learning, if ever High Learning is going to take place.

Questioning: The Way Across Open Space

In the moment of silence, a natural tendency must be resisted. It is our wont to fill up silence. In the case of organizations undergoing transformation, this usually means the latest edition of the corporate plan, or the pet projects of those on high that were never completed. All of this is presented in the hopes of giving people something to keep them occupied when they have nothing to do. The effect upon the process is chilling, for in the event that the people actually listen (which thankfully doesn't happen often), they will be deprived of an instant of pure creation, an experience never to be forgotten. And the organization will be deprived of the people's capacity to see differences that make a difference, which is the mother lode of innovation and breakthrough. In a word, everybody loses.

There is, however, one thing to be done, which may seem rather inconsequential given the gravity of the situation. Ask a question. *What are you going to do with the rest of your life?* Questions create space as opposed to statements, which make for closure. In this case we need plenty of space if the full value of the moment is to be realized. And this question in particular creates precisely the sort of space required. Raising the issue of "the rest of your life" suggests that there will be one, if desired. It is that possibility which lays the ground work for moving out of silence into wonder and imagination. The most helpful thing is not the answer, which all people must find for themselves. It is the question that sets the ball in motion.

This question may be asked in a multitude of ways, not all of them verbal. Words can do it, but as often it is a look or a touch. It may even be an apparently unrelated occurrence such as the smile of a small child, or the first light of dawn, which somehow communicates the possibility of continuance. No matter the source, when the question is asked, transformation may move forward.

The Quality of Questioning: Love The question itself is important, but how the question is asked is even more important. The necessary special quality is love. I recognize that love is not ordinarily associated with the rough and tumble life in organizations, particularly businesses. After all we are supposed to be hard-headed and bottom-line oriented. All true, but love itself has its hard edges, and without love, particularly in moments of transformation, the process tends to come to a shaky halt.

Of, course, throwing a word like love into the discussion can make things very confusing. After all, the word itself may mean so many different things that sometimes it appears to mean nothing at all. On the one hand it may simply be a not-too-subtle cover for pure fornication. In another moment, love is understood to be the divine essence. With such breadth of definitions I feel constrained to state my own.

For me, love always has two faces: a face of *challenge*, and a face of *acceptance*. Love as acceptance is perhaps the more familiar, and certainly the more enjoyable. It is not only nice, but essential to know that somewhere we are accepted for exactly what we are, warts and everything. In popular discourse, this face of love tends to be equated with "mother love," as in "He's the sort that only a mother could love." But total acceptance, all by itself, can be a big problem for a very simple reason. There are no standards. Anything goes.

Relationships built only on pure acceptance typically end up as mush. Lots of warm fuzzies, but no substance. The other side of love is essential: challenge.

Love as challenge expects the very best. It is not about being in a certain way, but rather being the best that one can possibly be. If the situation were school, the challenge is not to achieve a certain grade-point average, but rather to attain the best average for that person. It is all about personal best.

Neither challenge nor acceptance make it on their own. By itself, acceptance ends up with mush. And with no expectations, life degenerates to the lowest common denominator—or worse. Challenge, left to its own devices, is a monster, productive of workaholism and craziness. Nothing is ever good enough. It must be better, better, better. Not too far down the road and "better, better, better" turns to *guilt, guilt, guilt*. At that point everything pretty well falls apart.

But when challenge and acceptance stand in polarity (dialectical tension), really whole things happen. If we meet each other with full acceptance and radical challenge, everything we are and everything we could be is called forth. Talk about being whole people. Talk about full love.

Love like this is what makes the passage across Open Space possible. When the critical question, "What are you going to do with the rest of your life?" is asked in love (full acceptance and full challenge), it becomes clear that everything we are and could be is being invited to a new future.

But please note: This is an invitation—never a command. Only we can make the choice. For some the choice is to remain as we were, or even abort the journey. But that is our choice, and nobody can make it (or a different one) for us.

Wonder and Imagination When the question is asked, and the invitation extended, response is by no means automatic or guaranteed. Some of us (and probably all of us at some time) will choose not to press forward. We hope that the rest of our life may be the same, or similar to the past of our life. Even though the old world is now changed, perhaps radically, it still has a certain familiarity. We prefer the familiar to the possible.

But for others, the invitation is intriguing. The new and the different seem at least worth a little exploration. We find ourselves saying a magical phrase, "I wonder if . . . " I wonder if I could find a new job, a new life, a new life partner. . . . When wonder and imagination meet, Vision is born.

Vision

Vision is the picture of some future state that we hold in our head. But that is a very bland statement, for vision does not so much depict a new reality as create it. We do not follow our vision. We are driven by it, even possessed. There is an element of compulsion here. What vision lacks in concrete detail (plans, budgets, designs, and the like), it gains in sheer power. Vision is Spirit bursting out in new and powerful ways.

The power of vision is not surprising given its heritage. Born in chaos, baptized in shock, anger, and denial, vision emerges from the ashes of our memories, in despair and silence. Then, through the alchemy of wonder and imagination, it is transmuted into a consuming passion. That is power.

Contrast all of the above with the current fad: Vision Statements. Typically the product of a committee seeking to instill rationale and purpose in an organization that has seemingly lost both, the vision statement is a pale reflection of its namesake. More often than not, the vision statement lacks the one thing that could make it meaningful: passion.

True vision hardly needs to be stated, and is never the product of thought and effort. It emerges despite all efforts to contain it, from a place in our consciousness that seems to have little to do with thinking. Call it irrational if you like, provided that word is used without prejudice. Vision is prerational or subrational, the very ground and foundation from which rationality emerges. Given vision, you may figure out how to implement it, but you never think your way to vision. It is always the gift of chaos, the product of transformative High Learning.

chapter 6

Organization Development in Four Acts

AFTER VISION—WHAT? Presumably we get back to work, and once more the New Standard Business Curve begins to rise. New structure, new products and profits, all carried aloft on the wings of a renewed Spirit. True.

But there are also occurrences along the way to the future which are not described by that famous curve. Maybe it's just analogy or metaphor, but it seems to me that what we now know about the process of birthing suggests some useful insights regarding what happens to our organizations. The work in question was done largely by Stanislav Grof[1] as reported in his book, *Beyond the Brain*. Drawing upon physiological and psychoanalytical evidence, Grof relates what people have described as happening to them prior to birth; it apparently occurs in four stages. I leave it to Grof's colleagues to judge his findings, but I use them here, at least the basic description of the process, only because it has been helpful and suggestive to me in making sense of the developmental life of an organization. Herewith the Four Acts of organizational life.

A NOTE ON "OD" AND "OT"

Before moving to a description of the stages of development à la Stan Grof it will be useful to emphasize the critical distinction between *organization development* and *organization transformation*.

Organization development is a linear sequential process through which an organization becomes bigger, and hopefully better, thereby fulfilling its potential. Organization transformation is very different, and the operative word is *different*. Organization transformation involves a *state* change, and as such manifests as a nonlinear, discontinuous process, marked by radical ending (death) and radical new beginning.

Organization development occurs at those times when the surrounding environment is relatively stable. It allows for the organization, and those who participate therein, to become better at what they do through the addition and refinement of organizational processes and procedures.

Organization transformation occurs at those times when the surrounding environment radically alters, to the point that the previous way of doing business is no longer appropriate or workable. The choice is clear, albeit very uncomfortable. Evolve (transform) or go out of business. No longer is it a question of simply being better at what one does. It is now necessary to do and "be" in a very different way.

Organization Development and Organization Transformation may also be understood as practices, hence the field of OD and more recently, OT.

Several years ago the field of OT appeared when I, along with several colleagues, convened the *First International Symposium on Organization Transformation* in 1983. At that point, there was no small amount of excitement and confusion. The excitement appeared because of the novelty and possible power of OT. The confusion arose because of a perception that OD and OT were somehow opposed, or even antagonistic.

That perception, I believe, was a profound error. OD and OT are not opposed, just different, and each is necessary. OD is concerned with assisting the developmental process, and OT with the process of transformation. Different skills are required in each situation, and to apply the knowledge and practice of one in the situation of the other is to invite irrelevance at the least.

More recently, as the pace of the world has quickened, and transformation apparently laps transformation, the time available for development before the next transformation has seemingly shrunk to the point of nonexistence. For this reason it may appear that OD and OT have converged to the point of union. In practice we end up assisting organizations to develop even as they are on the verge of new transformation. But this convergence does not, in my opinion, remove the necessary distinction. It only blurs it.

And now, back to Stan Grof and the Four Acts of organization development.

BLISS

Life in the renewed organization, as life in the womb, begins as bliss. We might think of a small fetus doing joyful cartwheels in warm amniotic fluid. Something similar seems to happen in the early stages of our organizations. There is endless space to do whatever the heart might desire. New ideas are welcome because they need not contend with old ideas for attention. People, products, and procedures can proliferate without conflict. There are glorious and seemingly boundless open spaces in which to roam.

The possibility for innovation is without limit. At the same time, those wonderful innovations too often go without implementation simply because there are not enough hands (resources) to put them in place. Indeed, everything might stop right here, disappearing like a good idea whose time has not come. Alternatively, the troops and resources may be assembled to get the show on the road.

TIGHT QUARTERS

As new people and products enter the scene, the endless open space becomes a little crowded. At the beginning, the influx is comforting. It is nice to have all these new folks about, for many hands make light work. Shortly, however, the aphorism changes: Too many cooks spoil the broth. The pleasure of comrades on the journey is diminished when everybody is trying to do different things in the same time and space. Sooner or later, we have to get organized, and the system is born. Separate offices, new departments, procedures for running it all and keeping it all running pop up like mushrooms on a dark night. At best, the end result is a well-oiled machine. At worst it is a bloody nuisance as people fight the system, trying to get the job done.

But new systems may save the day, and it is perceived that better organization will overcome the mess. Whereas we used to just talk to each other, now we have to "communicate." The purchasing department replaces the quick trip to the hardware store for the necessary gizmo. And travel vouchers: sometimes it seems that it takes more time to compute the silly things than to take the trip and do the business. But this is called progress.

One fine day, space runs out. There is scarcely room to think, and no room to do anything useful. New thoughts and approaches run smack up against "the way it has always been done." New activities are shoehorned into odd nooks and crannies.

Meanwhile, the organizational effort proceeds. Reorganizations, rationalizations, all are aimed at keeping everything together. Systems are piled on systems, coordinating other systems, and new systems emerge to coordinate the coordination. Where does it end? Especially when it appears that the energy required to run the new systems outweighs the energy saved by their implementation? We have clearly reached the point of diminishing returns. If this were a baby, we would say there is simply too much baby and too little womb. It will get worse.

THE TOXIC SYSTEM

There comes a time in the womb when not only is there too much baby for comfort, there is too much baby for the plumbing system. The womb goes toxic. No longer is it possible to remove the natural waste products, and life must radically change or cease.

As unpleasant as the toxic womb may be, it has a purpose. It sets the essential conditions for birth. Humanitarian concerns might dictate an effort to clean up the mess, but in a fascinating way, any effort in this direction will only retard the process. Birth would be delayed, or not happen at all.

If we can accept Grof's description of life in the womb, it becomes clear why nobody would ever *want* to be born. Taking a trip down a small dark passage, to an unknown destination, is not attractive, unless the alternatives are infinitely less attractive. The toxic womb sets those unattractive alternatives. To stay is to die. But it is worthwhile noting that this is all part of the plan. The wonderful mechanism by which we come into the world includes a period so unpleasant that we literally have no choice but to be born.

I believe that the same sort of event occurs in that larger womb, our organizations. As the system grows, we pass from crowded quarters to a condition in which the whole system goes toxic. For a period of time, the emergency squads go tearing about the place plugging the leaks, and trying their level best to make life livable once more. Call those squads stress reduction seminars, job enhancement initiatives, conflict resolution programs, or whatever. They all have the laudable intent of detoxifying the environment, or at the very least, providing the organizational "gas masks" enabling us to remain in conditions no sane human would choose.

For a time, the detoxification effort is successful, but sooner or later the environmental toxins will overwhelm the inhabitants. Soul Pollution takes over.

The moment seems like disaster, but there is a silver lining in this cloud. The real problem is not that the system is malfunctioning, but rather that we have outgrown the system. Here, as in the womb, the efforts at detoxification are not only futile, they are counterproductive. One might even argue that continued efforts at detoxification (stress reduction, etc.) make as much sense as putting a pregnant woman on renal dialysis. The point is not to purify the womb, but to be born. Don't fix the organization, evolve to a new way of *being in organization*. It is time to go. The choice is clear. Evolve or die.

Perhaps it is totally fanciful, but when considering the larger organization of which we are all a part, Planet Earth, I wonder if the present environmental crisis is not part of a similar plan. No right-minded person can doubt that going the way we are, we will not (as a species) go very far. For the present, the environmental cleanup crews are hard at work, and in small places are making small progress. Yet the issue is not fixing the system, but creating a new way of being productive on this earth. And the problem is, doing that will require a basic change in what we hold to be valuable and useful. A change in the consciousness of what it means to be human, and what a full human life is all about. Conspicuous consumption must be replaced by *appropriate* consumption. Self-worth must be measured by contribution, and not by acquisition.

That change in consciousness will not come easily, and it is impeded by the fact that most of the ways in which we know how to engineer change simply are not effective. Given a nice linear, logical problem to solve, we are superb (Organization Development). But in this case, the fundamental premises are different, which means that our logic is without power. Somehow we have to take the leap into a very different way of being, and needless to say, nobody wants to do that (Organization Transformation). So perhaps Mother Earth is about ready to push us out of the nest. Into oblivion, if that is our choice. Or on to flight. Would it not be odd if the current ecological disaster were the most beneficial thing to have recently befallen humankind?

DOWN THE TUBES

The last act is both the end and the beginning. I apologize if the image of "down the tubes" is distasteful, but it is literally correct when speaking of the exit from the womb, and also common usage when describing the demise of an organization. In short, it fits.

It is a journey nobody cares to take. It is the end of the comfortable and known, in exchange for the unknown. For businesses it is Chapter 11, a fire sale, or just plain disaster. Call it the dark night of the soul, chaos, or the End, it all amounts to the same thing. The death of what was, which is also the birth of what will be.

With death, that is also a beginning, we come back to the Griefwork cycle. For a newborn baby, the first act is typically a scream, which initiates breathing. If the newborn had language skills, the first words would doubtless be, "Oh shit." And when we go down the tubes, it is quite likely that we will say the same. Even though the terrain to be covered as we go down the tubes may be unknown in detail, at least we know the plot. Once again we find ourselves engaged in the oldest story of humankind, the transformational journey from birth to death, and around again.

IS THIS TRIP NECESSARY?

The cycle of organizational birth and death looks rather like the Far Eastern Wheel of Karma. In the typical Western understanding, this wheel describes an endless circle of life and death, through innumerable incarnations, with no way out. That is true only in part, for given the will and the way, the cycle can be broken. The evolution of consciousness may proceed.

The critical step in the process is vision. And the central question is, *What is the envisioned future state?* If it is simply a return to what was, that is the likely outcome. On the other hand, if some higher state is held in view and the will exists to proceed, there is at least the possibility that the higher state will be achieved. No guarantees, of course. But the possibility exists.

The situation is not unlike that facing a client of mine after a terrorist attack on his plant. Seen from most points of view, the immediate prospects were not appealing. It was a mess, but a mess with choices. First of all, he could accept the end as the end, board the place up, and go out of business.

A second, more positive choice would be to enter the used equipment market and purchase replacements, duplicating exactly what had been lost. There is safety in this choice, for one would be dealing with known quantities, and presumably the time required for a return to production would be cut to a minimum. At the same time it must be recognized that one can never quite go home again.

A third choice existed. Take the disaster as the opportunity for a quantum leap to the next generation of technology. The risk is obviously far greater, for not only would the organization have to deal with the trauma of the attack and its aftermath, but also with the additional cost and trauma of introducing the new technology. But the potential benefits in this case were obviously the highest of all. I am pleased to say that my client chose to "go for the gold."

The essential issue in all cases is vision. What do you hold as a possible future state? Added to that must be the necessary determination to get there. If the vision of the future is that there *is* no future, the choice is obvious and easy. Should the vision be "more of the same," the road to that future is fairly clear. However, if the quantum leap forward is the vision of choice, neither the road nor the means come readily to hand. It is all new territory.

A similar set of choices confronts every organization once it has gone down the tubes and passed through the Griefwork cycle. When the moment of vision is reached, the issue is clearly set. Go out of business, go back to where you were, or make the leap to some new, and more effective, way of being.

THE STAKES OF THE GAME ARE RISING

In the good old days, whenever that was, the transformative process also took place, but over such an extended time that it sometimes appeared not to take place at all. The pace has changed dramatically and shows every sign of changing even more. What used to take 50 years can now happen in one year or less. That may seem a radical, perhaps irresponsible statement, but consider the case of the introduction of PC computer chips.

Were we to graph the rate of introduction against the increase in power from one chip to the next, we would see that, in this case at least, we are riding up the steep slope of an exponential curve.

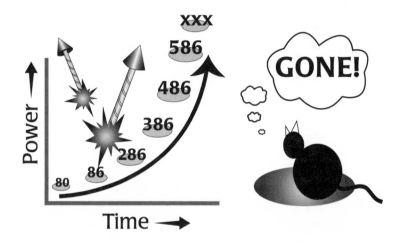

For all those in the computer industry, along with the rest of us who are affected by its evolution, the passage from one chip to the next generation is not just a minor improvement in technology. It is more like the introduction of a whole new business, and the consequent passage of an old one. Who would have thought that the once powerful 286 chip, heart of the Advanced Technology PC (AT), would be virtually eliminated from the market a scant four years after its introduction? The successive jumps from 86 to 286, 386, 486, 586, and shortly to XXX each brought new possibilities for software, for new applications, all requiring new marketing, sales, and production approaches. In short, whole new businesses. Those who sought to hold on to the old business approaches have found themselves holding the short end of the stick.

When described in the relatively neutral terms of advancing technology, the rate of change is interesting, even exciting. But seen from the human dimension, this rate of change could become, and indeed has become a holy terror for many of those involved. Plant closings, market downturns, layoffs, rapid obsolescence of skills. More than enough to turn your hair white, and cause nostalgic flashbacks to the good old days of job security. Some would restrain the rush of technology, but that is to hold a tiger by the tail. Not a very attractive option.

If we are to ride the exponential curve to our collective future, it behooves us to ride well. That means learning to negotiate the process of birth and death in our organizations with intention and skill, lest the Spirit become severely battered.

part **III**

The Stages of Transformation

THERE ARE STAGES IN ORGANIZATIONAL LIFE, very much as there are stages in the life of an individual, and I suppose in the life of the whole species. Identifying and naming those stages is a useful way of keeping track of where we are, and projecting where we are likely to go. But it is always important to remember that the stages are arbitrary and depend in large part on what you want to keep track of. The essential criteria are whether they work and whether you are able to see, and understand, in a new, deeper way. Rarely, if ever, is it a question of right or wrong, but rather of utility.

For our purposes, the central "what" to be tracked is the Spirit of a place as it evolves and manifests itself in new forms, for that is what transformation is all about. The forms themselves are like the crab's shell, good for a period of time, then discarded, but never to be confused with the crab.

A better image for the transformational journey of Spirit is the butterfly. As we all know, butterflies start out as caterpillars, then go into a cocoon (chrysalis), only to emerge with beautiful colors, and wings to fly. What we may not know, or always remember, is what happens in the cocoon. Inside, far from curious eyes, an incredible process takes place. The caterpillar quite literally dissolves into a sort of primal ooze, a real mess. And then, following directions coded somewhere in that mess, the raw protoplasm reaggregates, and what was once a crawling beastie now has the hardware to fly.

Put somewhat differently, and probably not in accord with the best biological thinking, the caterpillar goes to its essence (we might say Spirit) and then reforms, or better, transforms, to a totally new way of being. It is a journey from form, to nothingness, to new form. And there is no way of getting from caterpillar to butterfly except by passing through the void.

chapter 7

Stages Along Spirit's Way

PART II TRACED THE SPIRIT of a place as it moved from one way of being to a new one, the adaptive process. In and out of chrysalis, so to speak, through the cycle of birth and death. It is now time to consider the several forms that Spirit assumes along the way (caterpillars to butterflies as it were), thereby laying the groundwork for suggesting where we are, and where we might be headed.

Describing the forms of Spirit, particularly the Spirit of an organization, may seem a rather new undertaking. But conversations about Spirit have been going on forever, or so it seems. And some of them have gotten fairly detailed and precise. Most of these conversations have revolved around the Spirit of the individual, which in the East is often referred to as consciousness. The Eastern schema for describing the evolution of consciousness are numerous and complex, but basically break down into seven steps, or multiples thereof. The first and the last steps are essentially nothing or "void," about which not much can be said. However, the intervening five stages may be described very briefly as follows: *Body, Mind, Intellect, Soul,* and *Spirit.*[1]

As *Body,* Spirit is quite concentrated on the here and now. Physical concerns are primary, which is not all bad, but which definitely has its limitations. In quasi-contemporary jargon, this is the world of "Hunks" and "Dolls," those folks for whom the body is everything.

These limitations are thrown off, in part, as consciousness evolves to

Mind. The body, of course, is still very much there, but now transcendable in some ways. A major new element is language, which enables us not only to experience the world, but to talk about that experience, share it, and reflect upon it. Thinking, in short, comes into play.

The next level, *Intellect,* includes the preceding ones, but adds the element of awareness, or consciousness of our consciousness. Not only do we have experience (Body) and think about our experience (Mind), but we are *aware of experiencing the experience.* In practical terms, we begin to exist in a rational world that really doesn't exist anywhere except in our minds. This means that we can improve the quality of the activity of our minds and bodies by measuring our present state against some imagined future state. Life planning becomes a possibility. But it also means that we often confuse the constructs of our minds with reality itself, and come to the mistaken conclusion that what exists is "I." In a word, the ego is born, which as we all know is subject to being egotistical, or stuck on itself.

Breaking through the ego to rejoin the rest of the world is accomplished when we reach the level of *Soul.* My use of the word soul is not unlike Black American street usage, as in the phrases, "He/she has got soul," or "Soul Brother/Sister." Having soul is getting it all together and really being related. Instead of being "stuck in one's head," all elements are integrated: body, mind, and intellect. By the same token, the integration extends to the world at large. No longer the island ego, life can now be lived in genuine community.

It is noteworthy that each form of Spirit includes, and transcends, the preceding ones. Obviously you can't have a mind without a body, and the Intellect (even though it sometimes tries to get along by itself) requires both. When consciousness begins to operate at the level of Soul, which represents a real passage beyond ego, the ego is still there and still necessary. After all, you can't transcend something you never had.

The last stop along the journey of consciousness, or Spirit, is *Spirit.* I recognize this is a tautology, but how else can you say it? Spirit has become fully itself. Not that the Body, Mind, Intellect, and Soul have all disappeared, but rather, Spirit is no longer stuck with any of them. More accurately, Spirit can be any one, still be itself, and always know that it is more than all of its prior manifestations. Thus we can expect inspired performance from the body, enthusiastic mental activity, and spirited rational analysis. Most of all, Spirit can now be itself.

It is a little hard to say exactly what Spirit being itself might look like, for by definition we have passed beyond most of the forms at which we might look. Yet I think we all have intimations of pure Spirit, which occur at those moments of outstanding human performance that just flow. At such times, considerations of time, space, and effort do not enter the conversation. Maslow would call these "peak experiences."[2]

Obviously we do not have to go to the East to find a suitable evolutionary schema. The choice to go eastward is in part to acknowledge a substantial body of thinking that never quite surfaces in current organizational theory. There is also a deeper reason. Somehow most Western schemes stop at precisely the point where things really get interesting. Ego (intellect) appears to be the end of the line, and all we have to do is create bigger and better egos. But that, I think, is precisely the problem. As long as the world begins and ends with me, and my ego, the possibility that we will ever create the sort of planetary community necessary for our survival is limited.

THE ORGANIZATIONAL ANALOGUE

The following sequence is quite simply the organizational analogue to the traditional evolutionary stages of individual consciousness described above. The terms are not original. However, I believe they are used in an original way, which may occasion some difficulty. If confusion arises, I ask only that you allow the terms to function in context and not worry about whether my usage is "right." After all, it is only a story, but it happens to be my version.

My intention is to do a quick impressionistic sketch of each of the stages, and then with the schema laid out, slow down for a closer look at the stages of most concern to us in the present moment: the stage we are leaving, and the one we are about to assume. As I have suggested to this point, we are in an exciting moment of transformation. We know that the lifeform of our organizations is getting pretty shabby. Still present, but not functioning very well. We can intuit what a new way of being in organization might be like, but getting there is problematical. And so we sit on the fence, a very curious and painful position in which to find ourselves.

ReActive

The first manifestation of Spirit in an organization is ReActive, the analog to Body in the individual. That may sound quite negative, but I don't mean it that way. At its best, the ReActive Organization is electric with energy. It is primal, physical, vital, alive, and just about as aggressive as it ever will get. Fancy offices and elaborate procedures are not to be found, in part because of the youth of the organization, but it is also a matter of style. These are the days "out in the garage," where frills are not tolerated and anything unnecessary to getting the job done is either not noticed, or viewed with disdain.

One client lived out its days as a ReActive Organization over a Chinese laundry. Space was purely functional, and when new projects required a different configuration, walls were simply uprooted from the floor and reset, leaving behind the marks of their previous position. When I asked why they didn't clean up the mess, it became obvious they had never noticed it and didn't have the time. In addition, they rather liked the marks on the floor as a reminder of where they had been.

The central character in the ReActive Organization is the entrepreneur, the driven individual who brooks no interference with the realization of his or her creation. Not knowing, or not caring, why things have always been done in a certain way, this person seizes any viable possibility for the implementation of the "good idea." And any threat to its implementation, perceived or real, elicits instantaneous reaction. The personality and drive of the entrepreneur absolutely sets the tone and establishes the quality of Spirit.

Life in a ReActive Organization is truly exciting, and should the organization survive, this period inevitably becomes a major chapter in the perennial organizational favorite, "The Good Old Days." But survival is by no means guaranteed, and life in constant turmoil, self-generated or externally initiated, can become very trying. For some people, this is a chosen way of life, and when things calm down, if they ever do, those people will move on to some new garage or Chinese laundry. Alternatively they will stay and live in the world of the good old days.

When the basic mode of action is always reaction, the range of options is limited, and the amount of energy required just to stay in the same place is enormous. The strength of the organization eventually becomes its Achilles' heel. Constant innovation turns into reinventing the wheel. Life without constraint leads to endless firefighting. And reacting to each challenge, as if it had never happened before, requires a level of energy and dedication almost impossible to sustain.

The cost is paid in terms of employee burnout and a decline in customer satisfaction, both of which are interrelated. It is difficult, if not impossible, to satisfy customers with exhausted employees. And customers, once attracted by the energy of the organization and the innovation of the product, find that attraction diminished when the product is never delivered on time because all the organizational energy is devoted to putting out brush fires.

As a matter of fact, the ReActive Organization rather dislikes customers, or at best tolerates them. Customers get in the way. They are always asking questions, demanding services, looking for adjustments. If they would only learn their place in the order of things . . .

But customers pay the bills, a fact that may dawn slowly but inevitably. And sooner or later, chaos strikes. Not just the old, everyday, self-generated disorder characteristic of the ReActive Organization, but real chaos, tripped off by some trivial event (such as a note from the bank—something about insufficient funds), but generated ultimately from an inappropriate fit with the environment. Customers, after all, are necessary. It is time to move on. But to what?

The specifications for a useful future state are fairly clear. Everything previously done is needed, but in a way that is responsible to the needs of the customer (external environment) and the employee (internal environment). Good product, delivered in good time, without killing everybody just to get it out the door. It sounds easy and achievable, all we have to do is do it.

But not so fast. There is a price tag. All those folks who discovered their purpose in life through their ability to put out fires will now become responsible for ensuring that fires don't happen, at least as often as they used to. And those other folks, who experienced their full personal power in pushing the boundaries and constantly inventing the new, must now be satisfied with doing the same thing over and over again, at least until there is a modicum of efficiency and effectiveness, to say nothing of profit. A whole way of life must change.

Some significant number will choose not to make the trip, and those who do will discover that the emergent Spirit charges a high entrance fee. Let go of the old in order to discover the new. Transformation one more time, and grief must work its magic as the adaptive process continues. With a new Spirit, there can be a new organization, but no guarantees.

Responsive

Enter the Responsive Organization, the organizational analogue to the individual Mind. It is a genuinely nice place to work, and a nice place to do business. Walk in the door, and you can feel the Spirit. It is pleasant. Gone are the piles of junk from abandoned experiments, odd pieces of product and material stacked at random. In its place there is order, perhaps not elegant, but functional. Shelves and cabinets contain what they are supposed to contain, available for inspection.

And the employees have a smile. Not all the time, mind you, but more often than not. The harried firefighter of old is replaced by the courteous salesperson. Work is measured not by levels of exhaustion, but by regular time periods, eight hours a day, and five days a week, holidays and vacations included.

Good, responsive organizations are found all over the world. A typical manifestation is the mom-and-pop store—set in the neighborhood, knowing the neighbors, and serving everybody. In the United States, one might think of Radio Shack, or in the old days, Sears. The technology level is never high, but it always works, and if it doesn't, bring it back for a no-questions refund or replacement. Customers are truly important.

The English version of the Responsive Organization is the local pub, a place where generations have gathered to enjoy their favorite refreshment and each other. Nothing fancy, just good folks, good spirits (of all kinds), and a little something to eat if you are so inclined. Just like home, and maybe better. On any given day, you are likely to run into the same people, sitting in the same chairs (or spots at the bar), talking about the same thing. Change comes slowly, if at all, and a newcomer looking for their own place will probably have to await the next funeral. In the interim, God forbid they occupy the spot of a regular.

The Responsive Organization is a comfortable place and sensitive to the people involved: those served, and those who serve. The Responsive Organization can also be terminally boring. Just plain dull. Everything is as it always was, which is why people come, and keep coming back. The total focus is on the immediate neighborhood. The world beyond is somehow unrelated. Products arrive, are unpacked, stacked on shelves, and distributed. Nobody seems to know, or particularly care, where they came from, how they were made, or if there are any new ones. Global understanding is not a strong point in the Responsive Organization, and the basic operating premise is, Don't fix it if it ain't broke. After all, if it was good enough for our fathers, it is good enough for us—a truth that seems to remain true for very long periods of time. In the interim, it is good to be comfortable.

But the time arrives, even as it did in the ReActive Organization, when the organizational strength becomes its Achilles' heel. With a lack of understanding, to say nothing of curiosity, combined with a very narrow focus, it is all too easy for the wider world to change unnoticed. Events, which could have been prepared for with a little foresight, roll on until they roll over the good old comfortable Responsive Organization. Once more it is a time of chaos, and some important choices must be made. For a small time, the firefighters, left over from an earlier incarnation, do their job. And the responsible members attempt to be more responsive to the world as they knew it, but unfortunately the world has changed. Responsive organizations tend to go out of business, or at best be marginalized. Which is why really good pubs are found off the beaten paths in small villages and urban nooks and crannies.

Specifications for the desired future state, if the future is to be different from the past, are not hard to make. It would be good to retain the energy of the ReActive phase, combined with the service of the Responsive. But more is needed: rational, critical reflection, capable of sensing the winds of change and creating strategies to realize the emerging opportunities and minimize the potential threats. In short, *planning*, and with planning, the possibility of controlling the organization and the environment.

It sounds like a wonderful idea, waiting only to be done. But hold on for a moment. Here too there is a price tag. For all those people who found comfort in the daily sameness, and security in the assurance that things will be as they always were, the possibility of critical self-analysis hardly exists. And planning appears as a profound violation of everything meaningful in life, in fact it is contrary to their religion. If everything is always the same, why bother to plan? And if it is not the same, why bother with it at all? The process of transformation has begun once again. Some will make the trip. Some won't. But the Spirit of the place must find a new form.

ProActive

The ProActive Organization is a very different beast, characterized by such things as rationality, planning, control, and power. This is not surprising as the ProActive Organization is the counterpart to the individual Intellect, home of the ego.

At best, the ProActive Organization is truly impressive. A well-oiled machine, self-contained, self-confident, and powerful. Until fairly recently, to be ProActive was to be among the elite of world organizations, and to such organizations the elite (or would-be elite) flocked in droves.

This is the home of the MBA. Doing it all by the numbers, the MBA and fellow travelers created the megamonsters of the business world. Systems begat systems to control the flow of goods and services to the far corners of the globe. And perhaps more importantly, to control the flow of profits that returned.

Conceived as closed systems operating in a clockwork universe, ProActive Organizations created enormous wealth, power, and prestige. But they too have an Achilles' heel. The source of their power is also the cause of their weakness. Their obsession with control renders them ultimately incongruent with their environment.

The essential problem is that everything turns inward. To insure control, one attempts to close every aspect of the system. No leakage, nothing operating outside of official channels. All actions must be regimented according to The Plan. And the job of the manager is, of course, to make the plan, manage the plan, and meet the plan.

To a point, all of this works, and the obvious success of the ProActive Organization is a measure of that workability. But that point is passed when the desire for controlling a closed system translates into a belief, indeed firm certainty, that the system really is closed, and control, as desired, is possible. This is delusion, and the price of delusion is failure.

There is a word that aptly captures the pathology of the ProActive Organization. That word is *arrogance*. Walk into virtually any major corporation today and it quickly becomes apparent that for those who call that place "home," it is the world. Nothing else really exists, at least nothing that matters. For those organizations whose position has been secured for some time, the arrogance is tempered with something like the divine right of kings, and its corollary, *noblesse oblige*. There is something comfortable about all this, but there is no question about who is in charge, or at least who thinks they are in charge.

Remember, the individual analog of the ProActive Organization is Intellect, the home of the ego. And egos, as we all know, can become egotistical. Corporate arrogance and personal egotism are cut from the same cloth.

Every so often this arrogance finds verbal expression in some memorable ways, as for example, "What is good for America is good for General Motors and vice versa."[3] This revealing phrase was uttered by Charles Wilson, the president of General Motors.

The first part of the phrase probably would raise few eyebrows, but the "vice versa" put an interesting twist on things. Doubtless Charles Wilson saw little problem in what he had said, but for many it seemed he had gotten the cart before the horse.

Left at the level of idle comment, Wilson's pronouncement might seem just curious, but subsequent history demonstrated that there was more. For example, when the Japanese automakers started to bring their product to the American shores in a substantial way, General Motors, along with all the rest of the U.S. automakers, treated the new arrivals as minor annoyances at most. Rather like cockroaches inhabiting the dark corners of a house, they could be ignored unless they scuttled into the light, at which point a large boot would terminate the uninvited intruder. How could anything so small impact anything so big? Well we now all know the answer, and it wasn't the one that General Motors expected.

Arrogance, whether it be corporate or individual, has the unerring capacity to blind those affected to what is really going on in the world. And eventually world events demand their due. General Motors is not America, and it certainly is not the world. The lesson is always pointed and usually painful.

InterActive

Specifications for a desired future state, if the future is to be different from the present and immediate past, are not difficult to prescribe. Spirit must assume the form of an open system, operating among other open systems, all within the largest open system, the cosmos itself. I call this the InterActive Organization, and it is the organizational equivalent of the individual Soul. No longer turning inward to fix the system, the focus of Spirit turns outward to embrace the environment. And that embrace is not one of hostility and fear, protecting what is "mine" and "ours," as against "yours" and "theirs." For the simple truth of an open system is that we are all in it together. It is a world of leaky boundaries and interconnections, where distinctions are noted usually only in their dissolution.

It is also a world where chaos is no stranger, but rather the constant precursor of new order. Even as the environment must be embraced, so must chaos. This is the fecund ground of new creation, new organization. This is the world of self-organizing systems.

Under the circumstances, eternal structures and unchanging organizations are a thing of the past. The absence of change will become the major worry, for it means the end of life. In this context, control is a sometime thing. Here today and gone tomorrow, relinquished without anxiety and pain, but rather with something approaching joy. To embrace chaos is to lose control, and that is the precondition for birth and new growth.

Strange new world indeed. But if it happened, what would it be like? Among other things, I think we would find that the environmental crisis would turn from disaster into enormous opportunity. As we address the wounds of our planet we would discover new ways of being human that go vastly beyond the confines of a nine-to-five world with [illusory] job security, performing tasks that have lost their meaning. At a deeper level, we would know that wounding the planet is wounding ourselves. It is not just wrong, it is crazy.

On a more personal level, we would discover that in a world constantly in flux between chaos and order, the possibility for innovation and personal fulfillment is unending. No longer blocked by the way things were, we might playfully create the new. In a curious way work becomes play, and play becomes work. Not just a reversal of roles, but a blending of effect. Call it High Learning.

And for businesses, I think it would be wonderful. The day of the limited, finite market would be over, for in open systems there are no firm boundaries. Fighting for market share would become a ridiculous occupation, for a percentage of infinity is still infinity. Expansion and growth are limited only by our perceptions.

Sound good? Actually, I rather expect that to many it sounds like Pollyannaish chatter, suitable for nursery rhymes and fairy tales, but scarcely possible in the world as we know it. And that is just the point. Moving on, while attempting to maintain our present conception of the world and ourselves, is impossible. A change in conception, consciousness if you like, is essential.

Inspired

Before going more deeply into the transformative events of the present, we should complete the picture of the evolution of organizational consciousness. The InterActive Organization is not the end of the tale, if the analogy to the individual's transformational journey holds. Even as the individual may pass from Soul to Spirit, so I think the InterActive Organization will give way to the *Inspired Organization*. Clearly we aren't there yet, even a little bit, and given the pressure of the moment, it may be argued that such pie-in-the-sky speculations are of marginal utility. All true, but if it should turn out (as I suspect) that we are already well along the transformational journey to InterActivity, it may be useful to glimpse the next mountain top.

So what is the Inspired Organization, and why would we want to get there? Baldly stated, the Inspired Organization is organization without form. It is pure Spirit. To admit the obvious, this sounds like pure oxymoron. But I think we can intuit what it might be like, and indeed, there are moments in our common experience when we might actually "get there," if only for a moment.

For example, consider those times out of time when perhaps we had the privilege of attending the performance of a symphony orchestra. What started out as just another evening of Bach or Beethoven turned into a moment of pure magic. The stuffiness of the concert hall was transfigured into the elixir smell of open fields and mountain ranges. Hard seats dissolved until we hardly noticed them. Separate components of the orchestra were no longer separate, and it didn't seem to matter what was being played, or who was playing what—it was all one seamless experience. Call it magic, hallucination, or nothing at all, but it is what I might imagine inspired organization to be. Forms and structure just seem to fall away, and one is left with the pure essence of music.

If the symphony orchestra is not your thing, you might want to remember those moments from world-class athletics when something similar seems to happen. For me it was the golden days of U.S. basketball, when Larry Bird and Magic Johnson danced together. Yes, I know it was another clash between the Lakers and the Celtics, but somehow the score didn't seem to be the most important thing. Bird and Johnson pushed each other higher and higher past the normal forms of play. "Technical excellence" became a limp descriptor for what quickly became infinitely more than technique and a whole new understanding of excellence. Words just fail, but they always do when we experience the rarified heights of inspired performance. Or may we call it Inspired Organization?

And why would we want to get there? I guess the answer to that is pretty obvious, for I firmly believe there lies in the heart of each of us the dream that somehow we might transcend the formal limitations of our lives. Which brings us back to the good old InterActive Organization. As good as it is, and it certainly beats life in the ProActive Organization, it does have its limitations. Even though we may be constantly changing form in response to the multiple gifts of chaos, it's still form. Wouldn't it be wonderful to get beyond all that? Just to exist in our essence without the necessity to be any particular thing at all? And who knows, one of these days we may actually get there, but not now. For the present we have some pretty exciting times on our hands, and not a few moments of genuine anxiety.

WHERE ARE WE NOW?

With the stages of transformation before us it is worth asking where are we now? I believe the answer is that we are sitting, quite uncomfortably, on the fence. We are caught between the ProActive Organization, which we know not to be working, and the InterActive Organization, which sounds wonderful, but which comes with a very steep price tag.

Organization	Style	Hero	Individual
Inspired	Be	Nobody	Spirit
InterActive	Surfing	Everybody	Soul
ProActive	Control	MBA	Intellect
Responsive	Pleasant	Mom and Pop	Mind
ReActive	Charge!	Entrepreneur	Body

chapter 8
Over the Edge

IN THIS MESSY OLD WORLD, a few things are becoming clear. Change in the fundamental manner in which we organize ourselves is no longer a debatable issue. We are now down to the fine points: When? How much? and to what end?

In answer to the first question, the grudging consensus seems to be, "Immediately," if not before. The issue here is less about designing systems that are efficient and effective than about staying alive in these systems. On paper, our systems look marvelous. In practice the end result, more often than not, is vast amounts of Soul Pollution. Presumably we could run a little faster, give up another weekend, sacrifice another relationship, skimp on the quality time with our kids one more time. But who needs it?

So if change is inevitable, how much? To date the answer has been, "as little as possible." Words like *incremental, transitional, managed change* have populated the organizational vocabulary in this area. If change is necessary, as it seems to be, then the change process itself must be carefully controlled. This is a great sales pitch to harried executives who have enough on their plate and dare not face a genuine revolution, but with one problem. *Managing* change of the sort and order we currently face is simply ridiculous. It is necessary to move up the Richter Scale of organizational change words.

In order to make the stakes and possibilities of this critical moment in human history as clear as possible, as we move from ProActive to Inter-Active I will describe and contrast a few salient characteristics of each, beginning with the ProActive Organization. The characteristics are:

▼ The Attitude towards Chaos
▼ The Nature of Learning
▼ The Quality of Work and Play
▼ Structures and Controls
▼ A Desperate Search for Community

THE ATTITUDE TOWARDS CHAOS

The ProActive Organization hates chaos. Doubtless there are nicer ways to put this, but few that would reflect the deep loathing, to say nothing of fear, evidenced by the ProActive Organization in the presence of chaos. Indeed, even the possibility of chaos is sufficient to engender a wide range of offensive and defensive behaviors.

There is, for example, a keen sense of inside and outside the organization, which may appear almost a bunker mentality. Current employees are insiders, endowed with all the rights, duties, and privileges of their station. Ex-employees are history. Once somebody has left the sacred confines, few remember, and fewer still will admit to the remembrance. In extreme situations, paranoia is rampant. Anything on the "outside" is perceived as unknown, unknowable, out of our control, and therefore dangerous and bad. Healthy paranoia doubtless has its place, for the world contains some unpleasant realities. But when the paranoia becomes general, and everything outside is suspect, even customers and clients make the enemies list—which is definitely bad for business.

The attitude toward chaos is founded on the fundamental core beliefs of the ProActive Organization that it is a closed system with somebody in charge. Anything that would penetrate the walls and/or disturb the internal structure is perceived as evil, pure and simple. And the antidote for chaos, of course, is control, which becomes the Holy Grail.

THE NATURE OF LEARNING

The ProActive Organization, like all organizations, must constantly be learning, but its style of learning is peculiar and unique. It is all done by the numbers and constitutes what I have called Normal Learning.

Learning by the numbers is definitely orderly. Discrete bodies of knowledge are divided up into bite size pieces and identified by number. We have Professional Skills 101, 102, 103 . . . As each level is passed, new competencies (presumably) are gained, which permit higher levels of responsibility and compensation. This ensures that square pegs are placed in square holes, and that order and control are maintained.

There is however a down side. From the point of view of the learners, learning by the numbers tends to be dull and tedious. Original thought is suspect, and God forbid a Level 101 person should dabble in affairs properly considered at the Level 103. Everything must be taken in sequence. At its worst, learning and boredom are seen as natural companions. If you aren't bored, you can't be learning.

There is also a price for the organization as a whole. Creativity is simply off limits. In simpler and slower times, learning by the numbers was very effective. When the world held still for long periods of time, bodies of knowledge were in fact static. What was true today was true tomorrow, and presumably on into a distant future. But we live in a very different world in which even the "basics" are apt to change radically.

As you will remember, Normal Learning is to be contrasted with High Learning, which appears in those moments of paradigm shift, when old perceptions of reality are shattered and new ones emerge. It is very exciting, but messy and painful. Normal Learning is what happens after we arrive in the new place. The mess is cleaned up and order is restored.

There is absolutely nothing wrong with Normal Learning so long as it remembers its roots. There was a day when the normal was aberrant. And here is the problem for the ProActive Organization. The roots are forgotten, and Normal Learning becomes not only normative, but the only way of learning. A classic example is the case of Owens/Corning Fiberglas when the folks forgot the story of the birth of fiberglass, a moment of High Learning to be sure.

Given the genesis of High Learning, and the propensities of the ProActive Organization to avoid chaos, it is not surprising that High Learning is forgotten. High Learning was born out of chaos and in the midst of chaos. It is anything but predictable and orderly, and so the choice is made. Vague memories persist of moments when High Learning did break out, but as noted, these are usually treated as infrequent exceptions or curious anomalies. Everybody knows that learning and science are precise, orderly processes, at least everybody in the Pro-Active Organization.

THE QUALITY OF WORK AND PLAY

In the ProActive Organization, doing business is very serious business. In fact, having fun while at work is a definite no-no. Play in the work place is discouraged, although there are a few minor exceptions, which may be indulged only under strict policies of containment. One of these is the annual Christmas party. Of course the party can only happen once on a single day, and it is often addressed with the same level of serious commitment characteristic of the rest of the year. We *will* have fun, made possible by quantum doses of heavy anesthesia.

One may wonder at this strange behavior, but given the guiding principles of the ProActive Organization, anything else would be unthinkable. After all, having fun and being in total control stand in stark antithesis. Play, by definition, is likely to get out of control, and indeed it is the sense of difference and surprise that makes play playful. Anything else is just plain boring.

STRUCTURE AND CONTROLS: ONE RIGHT WAY

When it comes to matters of structure and control, there is exactly one right way of doing things—Mine! It is the right and duty of the Chief

Executive Officer (by whatever name) to establish and maintain the formal structure and control systems of the organization. This is sometimes done with assistance, but everybody knows where the buck stops. The flip phrase, "My way or the highway," captures the situation with clarity and precision.

Of course, perfection is sometimes eluded, which is why we find chief executive officers changing jobs with some rapidity. But the essential notion remains. There is one right way—we have just to find it. Someday the perfect person with the perfect structure and control will appear. In the interim it is necessary to make a few adjustments.

A DESPERATE SEARCH FOR COMMUNITY

One final behavioral characteristic of the ProActive Organization is the desperate search for community. This takes many forms, but perhaps the most tragic and pathetic occurs at the annual event when all hands are gathered to hear the CEO proclaim loudly, "We are all one big family."

The tragedy occurs because everybody (especially the CEO) hopes desperately that the statement is true. Pathos emerges when it becomes quite clear that nothing could be further from the truth. Clearly the speaker is indulging in a controlled substance or else "family status" must be part of some very distant strategic plan. Obviously it has little to do with present reality.

But, oh, how we wish it were so. The number of dollars and hours spent on community building and conflict resolution are uncounted and probably uncountable. Despite the effort, the hunger remains.

Of course, we can always pretend that community and connection with our work colleagues is a matter of little concern. After all it is only a job. But then we remember that our job accounts for more of our waking hours than virtually any other activity. More than the family we are raising or that raised us. More than the institutions of society that nurture us, or that we support. More than our friends from childhood, and around the neighborhood. Indeed, more than everything else all put together. Our job is what we do—for better or for worse. And when we find little community and less connection, is it any wonder that work itself becomes a drag?

So the search for community goes on, and it would be very nice if we could identify the guilty party who got us into this mess. Clearly some great "they" did it. Or did they? It could be that Pogo[1] was right after all: when we find the enemy it may well turn out to be us.

Not that any of us as individuals, or all of us collectively, ever set out to destroy community, but upon sober reflection I believe that we must conclude that the source of our disaffection is none other than the ProActive Organization, in which most of us have been active and enthusiastic participants. After all, isn't that the way work gets done, salaries get earned, life gets lived?

Neither by intention nor design, but nevertheless as an inevitable consequence, genuine human community dissolves in the ProActive Organization. The active agents are *control* and the *notion of a closed system*. I say "notion" because as previously indicated, I don't really think there is such a thing as a closed system, but our flawed attempts to create it are sufficient to loosen the toxins of destruction. In the name of efficiency, effectiveness, profitability, and above all else, control, walls are built dividing inside from outside, function from function, person from person. Communication is restricted to formal channels, and often limited to a need to know. Under such circumstances, genuine, open, shared livelihood—otherwise known as community—is just about impossible.

It rather reminds me of life in a zoo. All the critters have their cages, separate spaces for each species. Life of a sort goes on. Meals on demand with the residue nicely flushed away. But a zoo is a *collection*. It is by no means the rich, diverse *community* of the animal kingdom.

The analogy with a zoo may be more than a bad joke. For just as the animals are caged against their will, so also are the people in a ProActive Organization. Or at least it often seems that way. For example, people joke about golden handcuffs and other references to being shackled to their job. The joke sounds a little thin. Indeed, if the bumper stickers in my neighborhood are any indication, many people would rather be just about anywhere than at work. Obviously, these feelings are not universal, but that they exist at meaningful levels is beyond dispute.

Something is profoundly wrong when a significant number of people feel imprisoned by their organization. What is as bad, and maybe worse, is that there exists a tacit assumption that such imprisonment is necessary. Under extreme conditions, this assumption comes out in remarks such as that by one CEO who spoke of his organization as the asylum, with the employees as inmates. When the metaphors become jail and jailer, zoo and keeper, attendant and inmate, the whole idea of genuine community is in serious disrepair.

When the epitaph for the ProActive Organization is written, many good things will be said about high levels of productivity, the "good life" that it provided to many, the seedbed of all sorts of technological innovation. But there will be a serious charge against the account as well. The arrogance of control destroys human community.

AND/OR: THE MOMENT OF TRANSFORMATION

The difference between the ProActive Organization and the InterActive Organization is neatly caught with an *and/or*. It is all about chaos.

For the ProActive Organization the choice is clear. It is either chaos or order, in very absolute terms. Order of course is acceptable, and chaos not; therefore eliminate chaos. Naturally, this elimination never quite happens, but the intent and expectation is clear, as is the ideal. Someday, somewhere, there will appear a perfectly closed organization running with optimum efficiency and therefore great profitability. All external distractions must be removed, predictability is automatic and guaranteed, and the great machine rumbles on.

There is a price for this ideal, which we now pay. As the organization is closed and chaos eliminated, differences that make a difference disappear, or are overlooked. Learning in a deep sense comes to a halt, and innovation withers. Worse, the firewalls, external and internal, that defend the organization also isolate it from the external world, and internally its members are locked in hermetically sealed chambers.

External isolation reduces the possibility of rapid adaptation to changing environmental circumstances. Internal isolation destroys community. The end is not yet, but it is clearly in sight. As community desiccates, Soul Pollution becomes epidemic. As the doors to the outside world are closed, irrelevance is insured.

We know all about the Soul Pollution reflected in countless studies of burnout, stress, absenteeism, employee turnover, and various forms of addiction. But that knowledge is seductive, for it suggests that some sort of system fix is a possibility. And such fixes have appeared in multiple guises, called stress reduction, employee assistance, community building, conflict resolution, and more. Sooner or later we may recognize that the issue is not a system fix, but rather a decent funeral for an approach to organization that no longer serves us. However, that recognition may be slow in coming, due to what I call the *boiled frog syndrome.*

Boiled Frog Syndrome

According to folks who know about such things, it is quite possible to boil a frog alive without restraint. The frog will simply sit in the water until dead, *provided the temperature is raised slowly.* For multiple souls locked in the ProActive Organizations of the world, the situation is much the same. Given the isolation of the environment, insured by the firewalls built to defend the organization, information from other places arrives slowly and is always suspect (as in NIH: "not invented here"). With only a single frame of reference, this—whatever "this" is—is perceived as normal, and indeed the only thing there is. As bad as it is, or may become, it is what we have and there are no alternatives. It would be nice to think that we could turn the corner, but in order for that to happen, we must see that there is a corner to be turned.

Before the corner can be effectively negotiated, the news will have to arrive in different packages, striking more sensitive spots in our organizational anatomy, such as the pocketbook or some deeply held beliefs. We must also become aware of significant, useful alternatives. Pie in the sky is wonderful, but you can't eat it.

Actually, the early editions are already in the streets, and full feature stories are well under way. With regard to the pocketbook, I think when the history of this millennial moment is written, it will become clear that the major engines of growth and development in our economies were no longer the large corporations, those ProActive Organizations *par excellence*. While they were busily thrashing about in a boom/bust frenzy—hiring one day and firing the next, with the official press savoring every gory detail of massive layoffs—a strange thing was happening. The economy grew and new job creation plowed right ahead, more than keeping up with the losses. But the new jobs were coming from small organizations, increasingly headed by women. I think there is a message here.

Meanwhile, an attack on a firmly held belief is well under way, and the belief is the possibility of total control. In the old days, organizational control had a variety of tools and symbols, not the least of which was the organization chart. Recently, this mother lode of power and position may have fallen on hard times. For example, as a consultant I visit many organizations, and upon arrival, and by way of introducing me to the place, I am presented with the current organization chart. That is a very nice thought, but the comments that usually accompany the presentation are a little unsettling. The chart turns out to be out of date even before it was published, and I am assured (privately) that in order to get something done, you wouldn't want to follow it anyhow. Far better to see Louie in the Supply Room, or Melinda in Accounting.

Formal procedures are in scarcely better shape, having been replaced at significant points by what are called *workarounds*. Few people admit it publicly, but it is increasingly common knowledge that getting something done requires working around established procedure. Of course, the official posture is that we do things by the book, and so for obvious reasons nobody is tracking the workarounds. But I deeply suspect that when the organizational data collection system finally acknowledges the workaround and keeps an accurate tally, it will prove to be more the rule than the exception.

Those individuals who remain convinced that rules and procedures are the way to go for optimal organizational performance might want to check with the local union organizers. They have a secret weapon, and it is called "work to rule." This is not about skipping over the prescribed procedures, but just the opposite. The procedures (work rules) are followed in minute detail. And the result? Everything shuts down in a gooey mess. With such a weapon, having a strike is a waste of time. All you have to do is do what you are supposed to do, and the result is the same as a strike, or better.

We could go on with many similar examples, but for me the point has been sufficiently made. *If we actually did business the way we say we do business, we would be out of business.* While all of this may appear exceptionally bad news to those invested in the plans, procedures, and other paraphernalia of organizational life as it has been recently practiced, I rather think the good news outweighs the bad. Despite the obvious problems with the way we have been doing business, or at least say we have been doing business, the fact remains that we have been doing business, or as the British would say, we have muddled through.

The preceding examples may appear a little facile, but each in their own fashion has chipped away at a once-pervasive sense that there really is such a thing as total control. We might not achieve it at every moment, but we have had the idea that we could, and we were headed toward that goal. The impact of all of the above, meanwhile, is a definite change of executive attitude and expectation. Five years ago, I knew a number of executives who could look you in the eye and say, without equivocation, "I am in charge." Today I know of no such people.

To be sure, not many senior executives are standing before their Board or employees and saying they are not in charge, but in private moments they acknowledge that the rapid and complex changes (what I have called "raplexity") of the moment make it impossible to even think about what is going on, let alone control it in an absolute sense. Their acknowledgment often comes with a degree of wistfulness, and apparent surprise, that events should have turned as they have.

For example, one Col. George Norwood of the United States Air Force, who I believe was in charge of Strategic Planning at the time of the Gulf War, remarked, "Suddenly the world changed, and it didn't match what we were planning on."[2] Surprise, George, but I think the message is getting through. The time of transformation is now.

There must, however, be some clear alternative before we can finally let go of the good old ProActive Organization, and that alternative is coming into view, announced by the small change of *or* to *and*. Whereas the ProActive Organization firmly held (believed) that the choice was chaos or order, the emergent InterActive Organization sees things differently. It is chaos and order. Meaningful activity—creation, production, life itself—appears in the middle, in the dance between chaos and order.

BEHAVIORAL CHARACTERISTICS OF THE INTERACTIVE ORGANIZATION

"The times, they are a'changing." Bob Dylan was right. There is something new in our midst, although debate continues, as it will for some time, regarding its exact shape and the time of its arrival. But that something new is going on few would deny. I have called it the InterActive Organization, and although it delivers many of the same things as its predecessors because it includes its predecessors, it also transcends its forebearers and its manifest behavior is vastly different.

Attitude Toward Chaos

The InterActive Organization appreciates chaos. Love might be too strong a term, but chaos is now accepted as a natural and contributory element in the creative process. The disruptive moments (large and small), which create differences that make a difference, are seen for what they are: essential. There is no denying the pain and disequilibrium that comes with chaos, but instead of running away or seeking to banish the intruder, the InterActive Organization seizes the moment and looks for the opportunity. As old forms are destroyed or pushed out of the way, new possibilities emerge which may allow for a closer and more productive fit with the environment. This is called learning, constant learning.

At the heart of this new appreciation of chaos lies a deep change in self-understanding. No longer is an organization seen as a closed system which, under optimal conditions, may be tightly controlled towards predetermined and very specific results. An organization is seen for what it is, and always has been: open and self-organizing. And here is the wonderful part. The greatest blow to the old ego (corporate and individual) becomes a blessing. Organization happens by itself, order is for free. No one did it. All are natural consequences of the system itself. Gone are the sweatshop days when we had to wrestle the business to the ground and constrain it with iron cords of tight rational systems as prescribed by Scientific Management. We never *could* really succeed at all that, but now we don't have to even feel guilty.

Does that mean that responsibility has vaporized and that nothing remains to be done? Of course not, but the responsibility is now to care for and nurture a living creature, which requires a skill set closer to that of a gardener than an automobile mechanic, or worse, a prison warden. The gardener knows that, while much can be done under the heading of tilling the soil and providing water, at the end of the day the plants grow all by themselves. And it certainly doesn't help to keep pulling them up by the roots to see how they are coming along. We used to call that evaluation.

Actually, with the appearance of the InterActive Organization, the state of our being becomes of critical concern. It is not so much what we do that matters, it is rather how we are. Strange thought, but it is a strange new world when seen through the eyes of the old ProActive Organization. But all of this is getting ahead of our story, a tale we will tell in detail when we reach our final section: Part IV, Cultivating Spirit.

High Learning

The characteristic learning behavior of the InterActive Organization is what we have called High Learning. High Learning occurs in those moments when paradigms are busted, impossible ideas with possible results are hatched, and the air is simply charged with excitement. High Learning is a direct result of the appreciation of chaos, for when chaos hits, differences that make a difference stand out, and all of a sudden what appeared to be a well-trodden path is seen in new light. This is called breakthrough.

Normal Learning is still very much present, for after the defining moments of High Learning the mess must be cleaned up, and sense and use made out the new insights. The point is that Normal Learning *and* High Learning coexist, but it is the latter which provides the juice and excitement.

Even when Normal Learning takes over, there is an anticipation that High Learning will shortly break out. It is a continuum or a dance between breakthrough and practical application. The really good stories, however, are always about the moments of High Learning. As for the rest, it scarcely rises above the commonplace, for it *is* commonplace.

High Play

A truly outrageous characteristic of the InterActive Organization is its propensity for High Play. Not just trivial play, but serious play, which is at once fun and hugely productive. Having fun at work is definitely encouraged, and if things don't get out of control, something is clearly the matter.

For many people play and work simply do not belong in the same sentence. For the InterActive Organization, they not only belong together, but are virtually synonymous. The core matter is a serious one. When the defining mode of learning is High Learning, High Play is absolutely essential.

In High Learning new realities are perceived, which make the old ways of doing and thinking obsolete. The shift may not be as radical or dramatic as the move from an earth-centered to a solar-centered universe (or at least our small part of the universe), but the shifts take place, and any time old ways are questioned a certain dis-ease sets in.

The standard way of handling such a shift, or at least trying to make sense out of it, is to construct a new story, or more precisely a theory, to account for what seems to be going on. In the early stages, the new theories are pretty wild and incomplete, but over time, as experience grows, the new theoretical structure becomes more adequate. In the interim, there is an awful lot of trial and error.

This trial and error can be a terrible problem, particularly if any of the interim efforts are taken too seriously. The sad result is that people commence fighting for their theories as opposed to the larger good, which we might call truth. Theory, of course is simply a likely story told to account for the facts of the matter as known, and also to provide some level of predictive power. Like any story, a theory gets better with telling, and that process involves no small amount of adjustment, which in turn requires the letting go of one story in favor of another.

The arcane art of theory building may appear quite esoteric, but we all know the disastrous effects of bad theory, particularly bad theory held dogmatically. Consider the pain and disruption caused by the ongoing debate between Creationism and Darwinian Evolution.

High Play is the antidote for all of that. It assures that the effort may be pursued with vigor and precision, and at the end of the game let go of, in order to make ready for the next game. And woe unto the player who hangs on to last week's game.

One of the privileges of my life was to spend a good deal of time at the National Institutes of Health, where much of the biomedical research in the United States originates. While there I had the opportunity to see a lot of research up close and personal. To be sure there were a fair share of ego-driven scientists, but the best research was done quite playfully. Ideas and theories were tossed about in the true spirit of High Play.

If you want to catch something of the flavor, take a quick read through James Gleick's book, *Chaos*. Outside of presenting a marvelous introduction to the new science of complexity, it is just a great read, for he exquisitely captures the feelings of the participants, which was definitely seriously playful. High Play for sure.

For a more accessible and immediate introduction to High Play, drop by any good nursery school, particularly when amazing structures are being created from building blocks. With infinite patience (for a 4-year-old) each block is carefully and daringly placed until the structure rises above the heads of its lilliputian creators. And then the reality changes. It is called juice and crackers time. The game is over and a new one will start. But as everybody is heading for the door, a sly foot sneaks out, catching one of the lowest blocks, and with a most satisfying crash the towering edifice instantly becomes just another pile of blocks. Squeals of delight mark the ending and announce the possibility of something new and better, to be built at another time.

High Play, it would seem, comes quite naturally. No training needed. We have only to remember what we experienced in nursery school. And there is a larger point. I think it will turn out that most, if not all, of the skills and experiences of the InterActive Organization need little training. We need only remember, and perfect, what we already know.

Appropriate Structure and Controls

Structure and controls continue to exist, indeed they are probably stronger than ever—but with a difference. Both are now appropriate to the people involved, the task performed, and the environment in which it all happens. Change any one of the three (people, task, environment) and the structure and controls change as well—very quickly. After all, this is a self-organizing system where emergent structure and control is the name of the game.

It may have seemed, from some of the nastier things said to this point about structure and control, that both were somehow "bad." Nothing could be further from the truth. Without structure and control, organization becomes an amorphous blob, capable of little useful activity. The problem is not with structure and control per se, but rather with their arbitrary, and therefore inappropriate application.

When there is only one right structure as determined by the single person in charge (the CEO in the mythology of the ProActive Organization) it is guaranteed that a misfit will shortly occur, particularly in our fast-moving times. No matter how brilliant, educated, or committed that person (or small group) may be, events will shortly pass them by.

In a slower day, the same thing was true, but the margin for error was infinitely greater. After all, the world changed substantially once a millennium, or was it century or generation? No longer. Radical shifts take place in days, or less.

With the magic—and sometimes it does seem like magic—of self-organization, structure is constantly in the process of formation, adjusting to the changing environment, and control is exercised from the most appropriate point. The people (or person) in charge are those who care, and they are involved and knowledgeable about the task at hand. Change the people, the task, or the conditions (environment) under which it all happens and structure and control will change once again.

Genuine Community

Imagine an organization that actually feels like home. Not some idealized home where arguments never happen and everything is sunshine 24 hours a day, but a real-live home where you can just be yourself and grow. Founded in respect, nurtured by acceptance and stretched by challenge—that is a good home. And it also seems a reasonable description of genuine community.

Community in the InterActive Organization is not something you have to work on, train for, or design. It just happens as a natural phenomenon.

The natural occurrence of community may be hard to believe given our current difficulties in this area, but it starts from a very simple fact: we (that is, all human beings) *are* a community. We don't have to struggle, that is simply a fact of life.

Ridiculous you say? Consider the following. When viewed from space, there isn't a political barrier visible on planet Earth. To the extent that such barriers exist, they exist only in our minds.

Closer to home, it is obvious to all who have eyes to see that all *Homo sapiens* are virtually identical. Minimal differences in color occur, but all that is on a sliding scale, with no clear-cut breaks. Furthermore, the color of individual specimens is subject to change with the seasons. During the summer, many so called "white" people are a lot darker than a lot of so called "black" people. So much for color. It is true that some hominids are fatter, thinner, taller—but at the end of the day, they all look pretty much the same. Two legs, two arms, two eyes etc. Seen one, seen them all.

Last but by no means least, hominids can all make babies together, fertile babies that can themselves reproduce. In biology, that is usually the clincher separating one species from another. Any group that can reproduce fertile offspring is a species. All other differences are just incidental variation. For example, horses and donkeys are truly different, because when they mate you get mules, and mules are sterile. Take any fertile *Homo sapiens* on earth, mate that person with a member of the opposite sex, and ordinarily you get a human baby. At least that has been the experience.

Sounds pretty simple, perhaps too simple given our collective history of division, conflict, and discord. But it may just be that fundamentally, it *is* that simple. Such divisions as we encounter, albeit serious and painful, would then be difficulties of our own making—all in the mind (collective and individual), and minds can change given appropriate circumstances.

So we start as community, and then the divisions take over, at least that has been the continuing experience of humankind. Why would it be any different in the InterActive Organization? The key, I believe, lies in the four behavioral characteristics previously described: attitude toward chaos, High Learning, High Play, and appropriate structure and controls.

A gift of chaos is to create the conditions under which we can perceive differences that make a difference, through which learning occurs. With such a frame of mind, difference is no longer a terrible thing to be gotten rid of. Difference is what learning, and ultimately life, is all about. It is the antidote to equilibrium, and as the fellow said, "When you reach an equilibrium in biology you are dead." So in one short stroke, diversity becomes an asset to be cherished as opposed to a problem to be managed. Not a bad start as we attempt to realize what we already are: a community.

Next comes High Learning. When the atmosphere is electric with excitement and creativity, it is contagious, and even those who may be momentarily parked in a Normal Learning track can feel the energy, or may we say Spirit. After all, it could happen to them the very next day.

Ph.D.s in motivational theory are not required to understand that working with inspired people is inspirational in itself. But you can't become too serious, because that is when the fights, dogmas, and divisions set in. Enter High Play.

Our third characteristic, High Play, ensures that even things of ultimate concern are held with a degree of lightness. Not that such things are trivialized, but only that everybody understands as a matter of experience that maps are not the territory, the menu is not the meal, and that every good idea can be productive of a better one. Lastly, that there is no one right way. And at the end of the day, if we aren't having fun, something is terribly wrong.

No organization, however, can live for long on diversity, inspiration, and fun, although it certainly isn't a bad start. There will be a few things that we need to get done, and doing that will require structure, as in who is going to do what. And control, as in being sure it gets done— well. Were we to return to the days of the ProActive Organization, where the CEO determined who and what, while steel-eyed managers insured proper performance, that would be a real Spirit Killer for sure. But we don't have to, for in the InterActive Organization structure and controls are always appropriate to the people, task, and environment.

How could it be otherwise, for the structure arises from the group as it performs its task, which is the essence of self-organization. That structure may be hierarchical, a network, circular, some other shape, or hardly any shape at all, but its sole justification for existence is that it works. And when it doesn't work, let it go and allow another structure to appear in its place. Under the conditions of self-organization, structure happens all by itself, every time.

As for controls, they are all internalized. Who knows better how to do a job well than the people who care to do it? When people start from a point of passion, experienced as High Learning and pursued in the Spirit of High Play, they are obviously doing what they love, which pretty well ensures that they will love what they do. External control for quality and other sorts of standards is clearly redundant when the front-line people genuinely care.

Closely related to this quality of caring is the very important principle of *voluntary self-selection.* People are part of the organization because they choose to be. And why not? Where else could they follow what they have passion for and take the rewarding responsibility for seeing it happen? And if such an alternative place could be found—go there with our blessing! That is what two feet are for.

Unlike the ProActive Organization, this is not even vaguely like a prison, zoo, or asylum. For those worried about the loss of key personnel or proprietary secrets, a lock and a key will not do the job. It is better that people leave, perhaps to return with greater experience, renewed enthusiasm, and commitment than to remain feeling miserable, oppressed, and put down. This is not about altruism, just common sense. Unhappy people make for unproductive workplaces.

Now back to community. When people are doing what they love, and loving what they do, with structures and controls that are congruent to the tasks they perform and the environment they work in, there is nothing in the way. You can't help being what you already are. Especially when you begin with an appreciation of chaos and the differences that make a difference. It is just natural.

WE ARE ALREADY THERE (ALMOST)

It may have appeared that my description of the InterActive Organization is but another example of the flights of theoretical fancy, an ideal model that may be implemented someday with great effort and good luck. I have no question that we as a species are going to need lots of both (effort and good luck) if we are to complete the course apparently set for us in the realization of our potential. But the effort will be of a different sort than our present experience, having more to do with restraint and *not doing*—thereby providing maximum opportunity for being.

As for the good luck, we seem to have been on a pretty good roll for the past 100,000 years or so, and if we can avoid the ultimate shot in the foot, we might just muddle through. Not without a few tense moments for sure, but muddle through for all of that. No guarantees, of course.

And what is the source of this optimism? I honestly believe that we are well on the road to the next step of our evolution, and may in fact already be there, at least in the sense of having established a primary beachhead. Proof positive is nonexistent, but there are, I think, a number of suggestive signs.

Let's begin with the behavioral characteristics of the InterActive Organization just described. You may have suspected, with some justification, that I had fallen victim to the most Pollyannaish sort of speculation. But in fact my description is based on something quite real: the global experience with Open Space Technology.

Originally, the five characteristics represented my attempt to describe the manifest behaviors of groups operating in Open Space. Through hundreds of events in my own experience, confirmed by thousands of events facilitated by others, these behaviors showed up every time. Appreciation for chaos/diversity, High Learning, High Play, appropriate structure and control, and genuine community appeared every time the space was opened.

To be sure there were/are differences in intensity and form. Conservative, traditional groups in Europe or Canada displayed High Play or the sense of community in rather different ways than their more demonstrative American counterparts. But compared to their previous behavior it was clear that something new had entered the stage. When you watch a group of 160 Canadian bankers,[3] including the president and all senior officers, gathered to "enhance productivity in their bank," suddenly stand up in a circle on their own initiative, hold hands and celebrate each other—you know something rather different is taking place.

So what is the magic? One might suspect the unique skills of carefully trained facilitators, yet in the vast majority of cases, the facilitators have only read the book. Actually, there are multiple instances of people who have never read the book, but only participated in an event, and seem to do just as well.

Or perhaps it might be the case that facilitators of Open Space all came to it with extensive experience with facilitation in other modalities. Yet the truth of the matter is that those with the greatest prior facilitation experience often have the most difficulty with Open Space, for their prior experience is more often a liability than an asset. Such people typically do a lot and attempt to fix things with carefully designed "interventions," large and small. In Open Space there is little doing and no fixing.

There is no magic. I have to believe that the reason Open Space works to induce the manifest behaviors described is that the participating groups and individuals are "already there." Open Space adds nothing, it simply uncovers what is already present. And what is present is the leading edge of a new way of being in organization, which I have chosen to call the InterActive Organization. More accurately, of course, this is not a new way of being in organization, but rather *a new and deeper awareness* of what we already are—naturally occurring self-organizing systems.

Perhaps another explanation would be more appropriate, but I haven't found it. If you do, I urge that you let me know. In the interim, I choose to take the Open Space experience as a significant, albeit suggestive indication that the InterActive Organization is by no means the product of an overactive idealism. Rather it is a common everyday reality, very much present.

InterActive Organization for Real

While it is true that attempts to account for the whys and wherefores of Open Space initiated my growing belief that the InterActive Organization is alive, well, and growing, Open Space is by no means the only evidence. Indeed, it may not be the most important one.

For example, take a moment and identify those areas in your place of work where something is really getting done. Not the same old stuff, but innovative stuff done with a sense of creativity, adventure, and style. Where people actually enjoy coming to work each day, and at the end of the day, they may be tired, but not totally stressed out. Such places may not be frequently found, but even in the most hidebound, moribund establishment, they do show up.

With such a place in mind, consider how it is that they get things done. Not what they do concretely, as in produce a particular product, but rather their manner or style of operation. Looked at honestly, my bet is that the operation looks much more like an Open Space event, and therefore also the InterActive Organization, than how things are supposed to look according to the "Book of Management Procedures," which described life in the ProActive Organization. We even have names for such places. Tom Peters used to call them Skunk Works. Typically offline, out of sight, and terribly creative.

Now run through the checklist of behavioral characteristics of the InterActive Organization. Appreciation of chaos and diversity? High Learning? High Play? Appropriate structure and controls? Genuine community? I think you will find that they are all present, which strongly suggests that the impossible future is actually a very present now.

If the question is about "full blown" InterActive Organizations, the actual number is doubtless very small, but growing. In Part IV I will describe a small organization which has taken the plunge. To this we might add Visa International, the progeny of Dee Hock. I have no personal experience with Visa or Dee Hock, but his *Chaordic Organization* sounds very much like my experience with the InterActive Organization.

If the numbers are presently few, I believe that will change quickly and dramatically. A major driving force is the Internet, which has created a totally new plane of reality (a space) in which the InterActive Organization is particularly at home. More on this subject will appear in Part IV.

Where Are We Now?

So where are we now? I think right on the fence between ProActive and InterActive Organization. Fence-sitting is never comfortable, and our situation is no exception. We have come to recognize that our old way of doing business is decreasingly workable, and increasingly painful. At the same time we can recognize the outlines of a better way, proclaimed in any number of books under the general title of "Humanizing Work." So why can't we get off the fence? Why not let go and move on?

But there, precisely, is the problem: letting go. For to let go would be to acknowledge the fact that control, as we used to think we had it, no longer exists—if it ever did. And it seems that we will go to infinite lengths to avoid such acknowledgment. All of which causes us a great deal of extra work, and no small amount of pain.

The work piles up when we have to rationalize our accomplishments in terms suitable to the ProActive Organization, even when we know full well that is not the way things happened. The pain strikes because of a fundamental incongruence of our walk and our talk.

Consider what happens in the development of a new idea or process. If you look at what actually transpired, serendipity abounds and confusion reigns. Later on, listen to the official story and it all sounds like a model of orderly precision.

A workable scenario might be as follows: The design team had taken a break after a frustrating day, and stopped by a local watering hole for a few short beers. The conversation was random, but the Spirit was recovering. Suddenly Ed had a crazy idea. He ordered another beer and began to share. Just as suddenly old envelopes and bar napkins were filled with odd figures and crude drawings—and there *it* was. Wow!

But how do you explain this back at the office? First of all, don't tell anybody "it" was born in a bar. Do assemble all available literature that has virtually anything to do with the subject, including the report from last year's task force, which cost a lot of money and never seemed to get to the point. Convene focus groups and expert panels to prove what you already know. And failing everything else, hire a consultant.

In a world still locked in the language and procedures of the Pro-Active Organization, good ideas and fine work appearing outside the accepted territory have very hard sledding. If they are to be accepted, they must basically be retrofitted (I would say retrorationalized) to look like everything else. So, our walk and our talk go in two different directions, contributing to our workload, and adding to the pain.

Biting the Bullet

When do we take the leap, and how do we go about doing it? Sitting on the fence will not be tolerable for much longer, so how do we get to this wonderful thing called InterActive Organization?

One thing is clear, we will never get consciously and intentionally to the InterActive Organization in the same way that we used to get to new approaches, by executive fiat. In the old days, the CEO could stand up some morning and proclaim, "We will be a Learning Organization, have Quality Circles, practice Employee Involvement, _____ . . . " (fill in any other recent fad). The InterActive Organization can never be commanded into existence. If and when it happens, it will happen all by itself.

I think there are essentially two ways to go from this point forward. We can sit about and continue the pain and anxiety until such time as we are forced to let go by the simple fact of our exhaustion, when we no longer have the energy to continue the struggle. Following this route could take an awfully long time. And there is an alternative. Try a little Open Space.

It matters little whether you call "it" Open Space Technology, or something else, but the "technology" exists and has been beta-tested all over the place. It works.

If it is impossible to "command" the appearance of the InterActive Organization, it is quite possible to invite it. That, I think, is the unique contribution of Open Space. It is a good invitation.

Take any situation in your place of work that meets the conditions (high levels of complexity in terms of the issue, diversity in terms of the stakeholders, the presence of actual or potential conflict, and with a decision time of yesterday) and open some space. All of that can be done quite intentionally.

And when the space is open, notice what happens. Unless something very strange has occurred, or you still have aspirations for control of particular outcomes, you will experience the standard manifest behaviors of an Open Space environment. Appreciation of chaos/diversity, High Learning, High Play, appropriate structure and controls, and genuine community all move from the realm of "nice ideas" to "present reality." It works every time.

An interesting set of choices will then present themselves. You could do it again. You could do it better. Or you could go back to the way you were and continue the misery. Your choice.

When you run this experiment, as I hope you will, please remember, there is nothing magic about Open Space. It adds nothing new and does nothing that was not previously being done. It only enables us to see what we already are.

When or if we finally take the plunge and let go, we will find ourselves in very changed circumstances requiring some very different skill sets and new ways of approaching things. The operational manual for this new experience has yet to be fully written. But I think we can already see some of the major chapter headings and initial approaches. For a possible first draft, please read on. Part IV takes up a most important question. If the InterActive Organization has actually arrived, what on earth do we do with it?

part **IV**

Cultivating Spirit
The Care and Feeding
of the InterActive Organization

CULTIVATING SPIRIT may seem a rather odd phrase, but it is in keeping with the analogy to gardening (see page 118). In addition, the word *cultivating* is rich in associations. Cult, culture, cultivate all go together, and also share a common root, *colere* (Latin for "to till").

Of course, the word *cult* has a few associations we might rather avoid, but the basic meaning has something to do with Spirit. So if we were to put it all together we could say that culture is what the cult creates as a place for the cultivation of Spirit. It is not much of a sentence, but it does bring together the essential themes and elements we will be exploring.

The story to date is a simple one in outline, albeit complex in detail. When chaos strikes, Spirit goes on a journey (transformation), passing through multiple forms (ReActive, Responsive, etc.) until it arrives at a form appropriate to the unique time and circumstances in which it finds itself. As Spirit settles in, it needs a home, which we would call culture. The journey will doubtless continue, but for the moment there is a resting point.

Clearly it is too early to write the definitive operations manual for our new life in the InterActive Organization, but I think we have some pretty good clues, in addition to genuine experience from which to work. The experience has been gained in the ongoing natural experiment with Open Space Technology, buttressed by the nascent appearance of the InterActive Organization in everyday settings.

chapter 9

A New Way
Creating Space for Emergent Order

DIFFERENT TIMES DEMAND different tools and approaches. What worked well in the days of the ProActive Organization simply doesn't cut it any more. Our methods and approaches for that era are not necessarily bad, but they are now no longer appropriate and in fact usually prove to be counter-productive. In their stead we must discover new ways appropriate to a new reality—beginning right at the beginning. At the moment of creation, indeed at the moment *before* the moment of creation, what do we do?

Here is a scenario. You have just had a brilliant insight, call it a vision, about some new product or service. Clearly it will rock the marketplace and redefine the business. But, and it is a very big "BUT," how do you get from vision to actually doing business? The answer is simple, both in terms of statement and execution, even if the specific results are by no means guaranteed. But after all, there are precious few guarantees in this world, especially when it come to launching a new venture. The answer? Try a little Open Space.

There is no necessity to use Open Space Technology per se, but one way or another open some space, relatively safe nutrient space, where those who might care to join you may assemble. Send out an invitation, and remember to go for diversity, for that will be the rich resource out of which the new venture will grow.

There are some important Don'ts. Don't waste time structuring the meeting, and certainly put on hold that very natural inclination to specify particular outcomes. The structure will emerge, and the outcomes will be what they will be, regardless of your efforts.

Once the invitations are out and the space is ready, there is not much to do but wait. This could be a very anxious time, or you could let the anxiety go and get ready for your next brainstorm. Actually it is probably time for a break. Go home and see the kids, take a walk, read a book. Enjoy yourself!

On the great day, see what happens. Under the worst-case scenario, nobody will come, but that in itself is useful (albeit painful) information. It may have been a great idea, but not now. How much better to know the truth early on, before substantive resources are committed. Negative findings make positive contributions, as long as we listen to them.

A more probable scenario is that the right people will come. There may be many or few, but you will know they are the right people for a simple reason. They care about what you care about. Each person probably cares in a different way, but it is from that difference that real development can take place.

When the circle of caring people is established, emergent order manifests, automatically, no problem, on cue. And the circle is very important. Good stuff simply does not happen in squares and rows, or if it does, it is much slower and less satisfying.

If you are using Open Space Technology, immediate outcomes are in fact quite predictable. Within an hour and a half, the group will have determined the basic issues for discussion, created a timetable and roster of topics for discussion, and should be hard at work. Over the next two days (and for a subject as important as your new vision I would certainly go for two days) every issue of concern to anybody is on the table. The results of the discussion are captured in a set of proceedings, which are made available to all as produced. Come the evening of the second day, a party of sorts will doubtless break out as the completed proceedings are rushed to an overnight printer for duplication. On the morning of the third day priorities are established, related issues converged, and the immediate next-step actions determined. Not bad for two and a half days of work.

Actually, the predictable results exceed those identified. In addition to the concrete details of implementation for the new venture, something very important has happened to the group involved. They have demonstrated their ability to work in self-managed work groups. New leadership has been identified for the new venture. The emergent structure of the Open Space is in fact the emergent structure of the new organization. Doubtless it will change and require a degree of fine tuning, but for starters, it does the job. And most important, the collection of individuals assembled two days ago is now a group—indeed more than a group, it is a community, a community united by a common purpose, with defined areas of responsibility and tasks to be done. They have even had fun.

And please note, it all happened by itself. Nobody designed it, nobody ordered it into existence, or defined its mode of behavior. InterActive Organization is operational. It now remains to make it conscious and optimal.

MAKING IT CONSCIOUS

It is almost always the case in an Open Space event that the people involved fail to fully realize just what they have accomplished. At the beginning, as the group sits in the circle considering the intervening open space and the blank wall designated as their agenda, most folks, if asked, would say bluntly that the probability of something useful emerging could be measured in minus quantities. Fortunately they do not have long to wait, for doubtless their preconceptions would get the better of them. In what often seems a breathtakingly short period of time, the group finds itself moved from total skepticism to active, productive involvement. At the end, the group is typically delighted with the result, but quite unaware of just how far they have actually come. It would not be an overstatement to say that they have done what most would have considered to be the impossible. At some level, their degree of awareness matters little, unless of course one hopes to repeat and better the experience.

I have no reason to believe that awareness levels in the InterActive Organization would be any different, certainly in the initial encounters. But unlike a one-time Open Space event, the InterActive Organization will hopefully continue and improve. Therefore, bringing everything to some conscious level of awareness is essential. Not that everybody should ruminate on the finer points of self-organizing systems, which may be left to the academics, but people do need to know, if only in large detail, what is actually going on, so that they might reasonably and responsibly seek to do it all better.

OUT OF THE CHAOS, A PATTERN EMERGES

In an Open Space event, the group begins in chaos, or certainly on the edge of chaos. There is nothing meaningful there. It is all random possibility. Then very quickly nothing turns to something. Specific issues, concrete time and space configurations, and productive work all emerge. At the first it is rather vague and subject to change, but over time (two days) issues take shape, structures solidify—and by the end there are priorities and definitive consequent actions to be taken. In short, a pattern has emerged out of the chaos.

The details vary with each situation, but at some level of abstraction the pattern is describable and predictable. First, the priority items that have emerged may be separated out in a simple triage, based upon their degree of clarity. Some of the items are *clear*, and little remains to be done but to do it. We might call these "Do-Its." Others are *cloudy*, and although their importance is obvious, more information is required, in which case get it, which usually means forming some sort of information-gathering task group. Call these "Info-Groups."

Lastly, there are some items which can only be described as *cloudy and confused*. Their importance is crystal clear, but the appropriate consequent actions are clear as mud. For this final group of priorities, the way to go is open some more space and allow the process of self-organization to continue. Concretely this would mean convening another Open Space event, but this time focused on the specific priority issue. These sorts of things may be called *Open Space.*

Out of chaos
a pattern emerges!

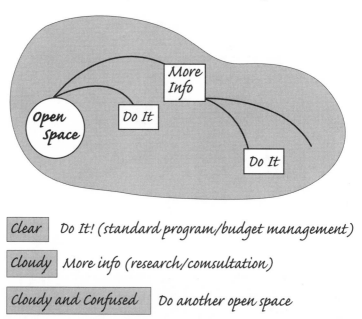

Clear	Do It! (standard program/budget management)
Cloudy	More info (research/comsultation)
Cloudy and Confused	Do another open space

Represented graphically, we can visualize a series of radiating arms stretching out from the initial Open Space. And the pattern replicates.

IT'S GROWING

Organically, for the organization is an organism, a network of roots and nodules spreads over space, and expands with time. Open Spaces beget Open Spaces, with related Do-Its and Info-Groups, as the organization explores its environment and tests responses for appropriateness and fit.

Predictability in terms of specific outcomes is virtually impossible, as are future directions, and size and level of complexity. It all depends on the complex dialogue between the organization (organism) and the environment, but the principles of self-organization underlie the process of growth.

It's Growing!!!

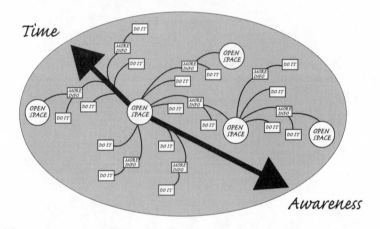

Looking at this graphic, you may well suspect an overly romantic imagination productive of an idealized image having little basis in reality. In fact the graphic emerged as I sought to give expression to the effects of Open Space Technology over time. In the fifteen years since the first Open Space in 1985, space has been opened thousands of times. Unfortunately we do not have detailed records of each event and its consequences, from which it would be possible to write a proper natural history. However, drawing upon my own experience, with confirmation from the experience of colleagues, it has become clear that Open Space begets Open Space and that the iterative process is productive of emergent organization. The graphic represents my best effort to depict what I have seen taking place.

A FABRIC OF SHARED MEANING

My picture of the growing InterActive Organization may remind you of the root structure of a plant with the filaments insinuating their way into new territory. After all, the InterActive Organization is a growing, living thing. Or you may think about a mind map,[1] that marvelously simple device for representing the evolution of a conversation or an idea in nonlinear ways.

The graphic *is* a mind map, but of a rather larger sort. We might call it a corporate mind map. If you start at the original Open Space and follow the lines outward, you can trace the development of thought and action over time. As people think and work together, a fabric of shared meaning comes into being. What started as nothing comes to life through the collaborative performance of daily tasks and the elaboration of common ideas. Everything coheres in a single vision, which becomes fuller, but never complete, as it is realized in space and time.

There are no walls in the InterActive Organization, at least none that make any substantial difference. To be sure, certain aspects of its daily activity do take place in buildings of one sort or another, but that is simply a matter of convenience or practical necessity. Perhaps most remarkable, the clear sense of inside and outside, so characteristic of the ProActive Organization, is diffuse at best, and often nonexistent. Boundaries are open, or in the manner of all living creatures, semipermeable, with a constant interchange between the environment and the organization.

Despite the openness, there is a sense of presence. Those who share the fabric of meaning find themselves defined by it to a large extent. They know, in an intuitive way, when they are "inside," and when they have moved beyond the unique powers and pull of the organization. To be truthful, the word *fabric*, although poetic, is too substantial. *Field* would be a better choice, as in energy field.

With the shift from *fabric* to *field*, another shift takes place in our manner of thinking. We find ourselves leaving the substantive, concrete, mechanical world of Newtonian thinking, and drawn toward the thought forms and modalities of the world of subatomic physics. Einstein, Heisenberg, and Schrödinger become our guides. It is not that we are "doing" high energy physics, or that the InterActive Organization is now to be seen as a quantum in that world, although doubtless all of that is true in some sense. Rather we may find the physicists' approach to reality useful as paradigm or analogue, with which to explore the rather strange new world in which we find ourselves.

Seen through eyes borrowed from our friends the physicists, a strange world becomes stranger. When an organization is perceived fundamentally as a field of meaning, an energy field, with no concrete (in the literal sense of the word) boundary, "inside" and "outside" become very relative terms.

Worse, or maybe better, we now find it possible to be "inside" a number of organizations simultaneously. Just as fields of energy may overlap or interpenetrate, so also do organizations.

In the world of Newton there is a guiding principle, that no two objects may occupy the same space at the same time. In the rather different world of high-energy physics, fields interpenetrate all the time. As a matter of fact, from a theoretical point of view it may be impossible ever to leave any field that has ever been. Apparently they just go on without end, irrespective of time or space. And so the energy field created at the moment of the Big Bang continues to envelop us, as does, in principle, every other field that has manifested itself along the way. Talk about the end of the notion of a closed system. It is all open as far as I can see, and with that openness comes the definitive end to control as we used to think we had it.

Strange talk to be sure, but not totally out of our range of experience, even in the days of the ProActive Organization. We tried to set boundaries, enforced by laws and custom. For example, we never brought our personal or family business to work, but truthfully we could never really leave it home either. And when our spouse, son, or daughter would violate all company regulations and call us at work (sinful!), we suddenly found ourselves in the field of meaning emanating from a very different source (organization) known as the Jones, or Kawalskis . . . or whatever our family name.

We actually had a descriptive name for this phenomenon. It was all about Spirit. We might say something like, "Even though my loved ones are far, far away, their Spirit is very much present." Sloppy, and generally unacceptable talk in the days of the ProActive Organization, but even then we knew what we were talking about, and so did everybody else who may have heard us.

As we become conscious of the nature of life in the InterActive Organization, not only will we come to accept and expect the incredible efficiencies that are now possible (like doing in two days that which used to take ten months), but we may also appreciate what used to be called the "softer" things as well. Warm fuzzies, by whatever name, are no longer an embarrassment, for Spirit in all of its dimensions can now take a rightful, central place in our awareness. It has always been true, even when we tried very hard to pretend that it wasn't. Now we need not feel guilty about indulging in such esoteric considerations.

THINGS COULD GET OUT OF CONTROL!

The universe of the InterActive Organization is a strange one indeed, especially when viewed from the perspective of its predecessor, the ProActive Organization. And for all of the good things that could and do take place in the InterActive Organization, there is a worry. Things could get out of control. Even if we acknowledge what I take to be the obvious—that control, as we once thought we had it, was but a figment of our imagination—the worry continues. If our organization now grows, as the InterActive Organization seems to, how do we maintain even a basic understanding of what is going on? It is all very well to say nice things about the freedom of organic development, but at the end of the day, what have we done? What's coming next? Are there some things that, even if previously pursued independently, would benefit from collaborative effort, and just plain old information sharing?

In the old days we had the comforting presence of the chain of command, buttressed by a formal communication system. News may have traveled slowly and decisions made with the alacrity of a fast-moving snail. But it all worked somehow, at least most of the time. Now it seems we have nothing. Everything appears to be happening everywhere, anytime it damn well pleases. That's a hell of a way to run a railroad, or anything else.

At this juncture, a certain nostalgia for the past is understandable, but before acquiescing to a return of the chain of command and rigid formal communication, we need to consider the cost. The increase in speed, productivity, and overall efficiency experienced in the InterActive Organization will be radically compromised by such a move. As comfortable as it might be, sort of like an old shoe, alternatives need be explored, which can accomplish the goal of useful communication without sacrificing the communicator or the essence of that which is communicated. As we become conscious of the expanding potential of the InterActive Organization, we must take steps to optimize its performance, and we may begin with adequate and appropriate communication.

chapter 10

Optimization

A Practical Way of Keeping in Touch

IF WE ENGAGE IN THE SEARCH for a fully InterActive mode of communication with which to support life in the InterActive Organization, our search need not be a long one. The answer to our needs is to be found as close as the nearest PC (or Mac). The name is Internet, or in its local version, Intranet.

Internet is the appropriate choice, and probably the only choice, because it provides an electronic environment, an open space, in which organization without walls can grow. To be sure there are those who have dreams of controlling the Net, but their dreams last only as long as it takes to create a new generation of software that opens things up once again. And yes, there is talk about creating secure firewalls, but any good hacker, given the time and the inclination, will find a way through. Because the Internet is essentially without limit and prescribed form, InterActive organization naturally finds a home there.

Where all this is headed, nobody knows, but the visionaries in our midst, like Kevin Kelly,[1] author of *Out of Control,* are striking out on some very interesting paths. What started out as an electronic mailbox has transmuted into an alternative reality, and from there into the cybersphere, a whole new "place" where things can grow. And in this new space/time, multiple creatures are being fruitful and multiplying like crazy, with names like Amazon.com, ebay, and Yahoo. Another name applies equally as well, I think: InterActive Organization.

If one were to ask if I could point to any currently existing Inter-Active Organizations, the answer is, certainly. There are a whole mess of them, and more are appearing every day. They do real business, produce real products, generate real innovation, but if we try to locate any one of them in what we used to call time and space, they have a nasty habit of slipping through our fingers, dissolving into the mists of cyberspace. Not all of these organizations understand their potential as Inter-Active Organizations, and few have yet to actualize it. And for sure, none would recognize the name. But that cyberspace is buzzing with new and very different organizational lifeforms, few could deny.

INTERNET: A NATIVE SPACE FOR THE INTERACTIVE ORGANIZATION

The Net began life as a super mailbox, and has effectively become a whole new reality. Seen through the eyes of the ProActive Organization, the Net is quite simply a marvelous new toy, which adds speed to our communications and reach to our organizational presence. Whereas we once had effect and presence only where we were physically located (Main Office, Branch Office, etc.), we now can be anywhere and everywhere all at the same time.

Seen with the eyes of the InterActive Organization, the picture changes rather radically. Instead of the Net being only an extension of our physical presence, our physical presence quickly becomes auxiliary to our presence on the Net. Clearly the tail is now wagging the dog, or it may be that we have a whole new dog. The thought is intriguing, and possibly outrageous.

Just suppose that the process of transformation is more or less as I have described it, both in terms of cause and effects. There was a day when the ProActive Organization represented a very adequate and useful form (manifestation) of our Spirit. In short, it worked. But the environment in which we operate has changed quite radically and the fit between environment and creature (us) is no longer a good one, which initiated the search for a new way of being. The result: the InterActive Organization.

The appearance of the InterActive Organization was quite uncomfortable for those still occupying the ProActive Organization. The newcomer was perceived as counterintuitive and somehow "wrong," leading to all sorts of denial, and often repression. But the forces that occasioned the rise of the InterActive Organization not only failed to abate, but actually intensified, with the result that the living organism, known generically as *Homo sapiens*, continued its evolutionary ways. In spite of all efforts to the contrary, the new organizational lifeform began to show up in places and spaces right in the heart of the old ProActive Organization, where it was treated with great suspicion, verging on scorn.

Fortunately a new territory was opening up, indeed a whole new plane of reality, now known as the cybersphere. This new territory was largely overlooked by the ProActive Organization, or if noticed, was trivialized as a new toy, and at best a sideshow. But while the ProActive folks were not looking as hard as they might, the new kids on the block found the new territory very much to their liking, moved in, and commenced to grow like crazy. The rest is pretty much history.

Finding itself in a totally accepting environment, the InterActive Organization has simply taken off. What it could not do in the restrictive, controlling environment dominated by the ProActive Organization, it could do with style in cyberspace: grow, expand, and generally feel its oats.

And just about now, a funny thing is happening. The side show is becoming the main event. Not that physical space and time, the hard facts and concrete realities so loved by the ProActive Organization, have ceased to exist, but they now have a new context, provided by a new reality. And with that change in context comes a change in definition. The once immutables—the facts, figures, organization charts, chains of command, the so called "hard things"—are no longer the only things. We clearly have a new way of doing business, and more importantly of being business.

Applied Internet

Employing the Internet in the service of the InterActive Organization is not rocket science. Indeed, all the needed technology already exists, and in most cases any twelve-year-old could do the job, or at least get started. Older folks such as myself may well have difficulty. But for the kids, its kid's stuff.

We start with the creation of a home page (see figure below). Every significant activity or event occurring in the InterActive Organization, which we might call My-Business Inc., is represented by a URL button, which takes you to the relevant documentation.

We have round ovals for the several Open Space events. Click on the button and you are taken to a full set of the proceedings generated at that Open Space. Should the Open Space still be in progress, you will get whatever they have produced to that point. If the event has concluded, you will also see the priority ranking of issues discussed, the convergence patterns of related issues, and an indication of immediate next steps, defined under the general headings of "Do It," "More Info," and "Open Space."

Each next step, as it is taken, has its own URL. Squares for More-Infos, triangles for Do-Its, and of course more circles for the emergent Open Spaces. Now it is time to start surfing. Click on a triangle and you will find out what the folks are doing with the Do-Its. If it is a new product, you will find out when it will be released, or what the current sales record is. Hit a square, and you will discover how the Information Task Group is making out. What do they know? What do they need to know? And when will their work be complete?

With the addition of a few currently available bells and whistles, such as conferencing capability and a good search engine, things get much more interesting. With conference capability, anybody anywhere can not only ask for further information, but provide it as well. Physical proximity to a piece of ongoing work is no longer a necessity.

A good search engine allows all members of the organization to find needed information, partners for new ventures, and valuable "lessons learned"—the successes *and* the failures. Although every organization loves to have its success stories, hearing the bad news as well can be exceedingly valuable. There is no point in doing again what we already know won't work.

Maintenance

There are a few practical details to be taken care of. The first is the maintenance of the system.

Effective operation of the glorious electronic environment described obviously depends upon all participants doing their part to keep the system updated and maintained. Information about current projects, ongoing task groups, and new Open Space will only be available if the folks involved take the necessary time to put the right stuff in the right places. And suppose they don't, or to ask the same question in a different way, why would they want to?

The answer to the first form of the question is simple and straightforward. If folks don't participate, the organization, at least its electronic manifestation, will die. And forcing these folks to do what they don't want to do will achieve the same result. Information provided against the will of the provider is often of questionable quality. In the old phrase, "Garbage in, garbage out," and everything will shut down. Which leads us naturally to the second form of the question: why would they want to?

The answer is embarrassingly simple. They care. A fundamental principle of the InterActive Organization is self-selection. People are there because they care to be there. Their reasons for caring may be multiple, including but not limited to the necessity for earning a living.

High levels of caring are sustained only when people are proud of their work to the point that they want to share it, open to innovation to the point that they are constantly looking for relevant information and opportunities, and committed to the vision of the organization to the point that they will go the extra mile to insure its realization. All of these elements are critical, and none of them come naturally from the electronic environment, nor are they automatically present over time. Something more is required, something called integrity, discipline, competence, a clear sense of purpose, in short—values.

Positive values constitute the heart and soul of the InterActive Organization. There is no substitute for their presence, and there is no way to "command" them into existence. We will turn to all of that in the next chapter, but for the moment, we need to make a few additional comments and observations on the electronic environment, especially on the subject of security.

Security

The issues of security and proprietary interests do not disappear in the InterActive Organization, for a very simple reason: not everybody is nice. Even though it would be marvelous should love and light break out in full abundance, the likelihood of that occurrence is small. Some folks are just plain nasty.

The answer to the security issue was much easier in the days of the ProActive Organization. With a closed system, we simply locked everything up tight. Bar the doors and windows, issue security passes, and set the guards. The fact that things didn't always work out as intended was mitigated by an underlying certainty that we at least knew the right way. Given a leak, close it off. If not now, then as soon as possible.

Life in the InterActive Organization is rather more complex. Not only do we have the inevitable glitches in security due to mechanical failure, but there is a deeper concern driven by the fact that were we to be totally successful in closing the system, the system would die. This is true of any organism. Deprived of air and food and restricted in terms of the elimination of waste, the prognosis is anything but good. The InterActive Organization, as an organism, is no exception. Thus there is a delicate trade-off between openness and closure. Too much either way, and we are in deep trouble.

This is probably the crunch point, the moment when we have to bite the bullet and come fully to terms with the new reality we experience in the InterActive Organization. And it is all about chaos and control. To the extent that we persist in viewing the InterActive Organization with eyes developed in our prior incarnation, we create an impossible situation. If security is seen only in terms of the preservation of the forms and structures of the organization, the intervention of chaos is the enemy, and absolute control the answer. But chaos, we have discovered, is the opening to innovation, and control as we knew it an illusion. Not a happy situation. We need different eyes.

The good news is that in the InterActive Organization the focal point of identity has shifted from forms to process. The specific structures of organization constantly change in response to variance in the people involved, the tasks performed, and the environment in which it all takes place. The function of security also shifts from protection of the structures to protection of the process. The structures may come and go, but when the process ceases, it's all over.

The core process, of course, is self-organization, and the critical elements to be maintained are the essential preconditions necessary for self-organization to take place. From Stuart Kauffman, we learned these elements to be:

- ▼ A relatively safe nutrient environment
- ▼ A high level of diversity
- ▼ Sparse prior connections
- ▼ A drive toward improvement
- ▼ Being on the edge of chaos

Thus security turns out to be much more about keeping things open rather than about closing them down. The world is certainly a different place when a major function of security is to ensure the presence of chaos.

It may be considerably easier to comprehend the new nature of security in more practical terms. Today, leading organizations do so through innovation, and they are the survivors and thrivers. This is not always the case, for some organizational survivors manage to hide out at the margins, but life at the margins tends to be marginal. For the major players, innovation is the way, and unfortunately last week's innovation usually appears ho-hum today. The net effect is that products and services on the shelves are virtually outdated, even before introduction. The future lies in items that are just now being invented, or have yet to be invented. Further, the odds favor the innovator and not the copier, who by definition is always a step behind.

Does that mean that we should actually give our new products away? Strange as it may seem, the answer is, sometimes. When more energy is expended on protecting the product than on innovating new ones, it may well be the best policy to give the product away and move on. This of course is exactly what happened in the Internet browser arena. Both Microsoft and Netscape do just that.[2]

But *sometimes* is not all the time. All other things being equal, the longer a given product or service is proprietary and secure, the greater the return on the original investment—which is why things like trademarks and copyrights are very useful. But there is a necessary balance, and not a single right answer. Trade-offs and choices must be made.

When we turn to the issue of internal security in the InterActive Organization, things become markedly easier. The guardian is no longer a need-to-know information policy enforced by hermetically sealed "safe-rooms," from which no useful ideas are allowed to escape, but rather an internalized set of safeguards arising from the fact that the people involved *care*. They care about themselves, they care about their fellows, and they care about the organization of which they are a part. And nobody hurts something they truly care about.

And what do we do with the rogues, as doubtless rogues will occasionally appear? In the first instance, we help them to see a better way, and failing that we provide an opportunity for them to exercise the law of two feet. But one thing that should not be done is what has often been done in the ProActive Organization, making the whole thing so rogue-proof that even the good guys suffer.

PLANNING, DOING, TRAINING

Other benefits of our home page will reveal themselves through experience. These benefits include the close integration of what in my opinion are the three elemental functions of any organization: planning, doing, and training, and not necessarily in that order.

Planning is figuring out where we are and where we want to move to. Doing is pretty much what it says, producing the goods or services. And training is learning to do it all better. Under optimal circumstances, each element should be connected to the others. But very often, under the press of business, things separate out. It would be very nice if everybody could sing from the same page, even if the parts are quite different.

Our home page can be such a page. Looked at from one point of view, it is an operational status report, showing what is actually being done. Change the point of view, and it is a planning document, showing where we have been, and suggesting where we might go. And finally, it is the most complete curriculum we are ever likely to produce. For new employees, some time surfing the home page will bring them up to date on total operations and show them clearly where they might fit in. For old hands, there is all the information necessary to assess current practice and figure out how to do it better. With the help of a good search engine, the best practices and available expertise may be quickly identified, regardless of where either might be located, virtually or for real. With best practices and identified expertise in hand, designing more formal training modules becomes relatively simple.

We should note in passing that training in the InterActive Organization becomes very much a self-directed learning environment. Adult educators have for years agreed that such an environment is optimal, although it has most often been a great idea that never quite happened. But the logic of the situation is inescapable, as can easily be demonstrated by a little self-reflection. Is it not true that you learn best when you are interested in the subject and encouraged to learn in a manner suitable to yourself and at a pace that fits your own needs? There is an old saying that when the student is ready, the teacher will appear. Our home page increases the possibility that such learning will take place.

Self-directed learning, of course, presupposes that learners will take responsibility for their own learning. Strange idea, especially as we come out of the ProActive Organization, where the assumption was tacitly made if not formally stated, that people just wouldn't learn new things unless coerced. Learning, after all, was supposed to be hard work, usually unpleasant, and boring. Fortunately, in the InterActive Organization the environment has changed. High Learning and High Play are now present—if not all the time, then sufficiently often to set the flavor. Add the presence of genuine community and we have the ingredients for a genuine learning community, or we might say Learning Organization. No longer the product of careful design and forceful implementation, it is rather the natural consequence of self-organization. After all, self-organizing systems do learn. That is their nature.

chapter 11
Sustaining the Integrity of Spirit

THE ISSUE OF KEEPING THINGS TOGETHER in the InterActive Organization goes much deeper than matters of information sharing necessary for collaborative effort. At root, it is a question of integrity, and not just system integrity, as in insuring the conscious and continuing connection between activities and elements of the organization. It is also moral integrity, as in shared values, and most particularly shared positive values.

At the end of the day, the organization will live or die depending on the strength and quality of its values. Is this a place where people care to be, where they feel the freedom to follow responsibly what has heart and meaning for them? Do they feel respected, treated with dignity? Is there room for real differences, allowing for innovation? Does the inevitable conflict arising from differences lead to deeper solutions, or simply to dissolution? If the answer to these questions is yes, organizational life can be rich, full, and long lasting. A negative answer will quickly produce the kind of life circumstances Thomas Hobbes described as "nasty, brutish, and short."

The ProActive Organization also had such issues, but their resolution, at least conceptually, was infinitely easier. With the strong walls of a closed system and a form of governance not terribly far from dictatorship, one simply barred the doors and windows, issued the value statement, and demanded adherence. The harshness implied was often miti-

gesture toward participatory development of the value
the end, the buck stopped where it always stopped,
quivalent. The fact that the whole system was, to some
based on a fundamental disrespect, or at best disregard
ᴏ. ᴡʜᴀᴛ ᴛne people in the organization might be wanting or needing,
was conveniently overlooked, as was the value statement.

The InterActive Organization is a very different creature. The organizational boundaries are semipermeable and often barely existent. Command and control is understood to be what it always was, illusory. But the need for integrity of a moral sort is, if anything, more important. Under such circumstances, executive proclamation of the Value Statement will scarcely do the job. We will have to dig deeper.

INTO THE REALM OF CULTURE AND MYTH

Digging deeper requires going below the surface manifestations of organizational life, the budgets, departments, plants, and facilities, down to the soul of the organization. This is the realm of culture and myth.

Not very long ago the notion that organizations, most particularly businesses, might have a culture was an unthinkable one. For example, in 1979 I submitted a paper on the subject to a well known and respected journal, only to have it rejected with the note that the whole idea of culture in organizations was so far out as to be not useful. Times have changed, and indeed the mention of organizational culture is now perhaps more commonplace than organization transformation. But just as transformation is often trivialized as a slightly enhanced version of what we used to call *change*, so culture, more often than not, is reduced to external artifacts, the bits and pieces as it were. The special language, the odd rituals, the corporate totems (the Pink Panther for Owens/Corning Fiberglas for example) are all significant, but not sufficient for an understanding of an organization's culture. We have to go deeper, I believe.

Edward T. Hall, a noted anthropologist, leads us in the right direction when he says very simply, "Culture is man's medium."[1] We may forgive Hall's gender-specific reference, and change "man" to humankind, but if his language is archaic to us today, the thought is original. Culture in its essence is more than the bits and pieces, indeed more than the sum of all the bits and pieces. Culture is the *ethos* in which humankind in all its variety dwells. It is the peculiar space–time continuum which at once defines, and is defined by the residents.

Culture is actually beyond space and time, for it *creates* space and time, at least it creates the special sense of space and time bounding the lives of those who exist within it. Thus we have multiple cultures, and we know that because when we as outsiders enter a new culture, the sense of space and time, and all the things that represent that space–time continuum, change. Time is a very different thing in North and South America. There is not a "right time" or a "wrong time," only culture-specific time. Space too changes with culture change. What is "just down the road" in the culture of Texas lies practically at the end of the earth for the residents of New York.

And things become even stranger. Past, present, and future become all mixed up. Although people may talk about the past, acknowledge the present, and dream about the future, at the level of culture, there is really only one thing: now. And the now may be driven and shaped by what in other situations we would call the past or the future. People and events from thousands of years ago may be infinitely more powerful now than the happenings of last week. Or some future dream, never realized, but just hanging there timelessly, may fill the now with meaning and in so doing, define daily behaviors. At some point we may come to realize that the clock, that apparent dictator of order and progress in the Western world, is an interesting curiosity and at best, a useful benchmarking tool. But it has no power to start or end anything, unless we give it that power. In the realm of culture, whenever it starts is the right time.

A Theoretical Framework for Culture and Myth

Before going further, it will help to lay out a conceptual framework in which the phenomena enumerated above may make some sense. Note that this is a conceptual framework, or more properly a theoretical construct. As such, questions of truth or falsity are mostly beside the point. Adequacy is determined by the theory's capacity to account for the elements of common experience and to enable working with those elements in useful, productive, and at some level, predictive ways. Can there be other theories? Of course, but they must be judged by the same standards. Ultimately, my standard is that the theory enable useful practice in the everyday working world.

Laying out the elements of this theory can mercifully be done quickly, but it will probably require close attention on your part. It will also require that you take things one step at a time, and suspend critical judgement until all the pieces are on the table. At that point we will be able to put it all together, and most importantly put it to work in the setting of a real, live, messy, everyday organization. In the interest of brevity, many of the supporting details are sacrificed. They may be found in my first book, *Spirit: Transformation and Development in Organizations.*[2]

There are three fundamental propositions, which are briefly described, and then applied.

1. Culture is the dynamic field in which Spirit dwells.
2. The power, focus, and integrity of culture is maintained by the stories we tell. Their proper name is myth.
3. Myth manifests Spirit in time and space.

Culture Is the Dynamic Field in Which Spirit Dwells You will note that I have expanded and modified Hall's brief dictum. "Medium" has been changed to "dynamic field," and *Spirit* has been added. Although I believe myself to be moving in the direction Hall indicated, I must accept full responsibility for what comes next, albeit with many thanks to Edward T.

The change from *medium* to *dynamic* field brings us in line with our previous discussion of the emergence of the InterActive Organization, which we described in terms of a growing field of meaning. With the use of the word field, we move very intentionally into the thought forms of high-energy physics, not to do physics, but to borrow its way of thinking. Out of the world of Newton, into the world of the Quantum—culture is to be seen no longer as the bits and pieces of experience, but rather as a field of energy, or as I would prefer to say, Spirit. The operative words change from "things" and "parts" to "forces" and "flow." Space and time transmute to space–time, the relativistic and, to an extent arbitrary, determination of position and movement dependant upon context. My space–time can be very different from your space–time if we exist in different fields, or as here, cultures. It is not about right and wrong abstractly or universally, but rather about context and culture. Everybody sees everything from their own point of view.

Things can very quickly become confused, messy, and ultimately overwhelming. It is all very well to exist in a field of cultural relativity for a theoretical moment, but very quickly we will find ourselves looking for some sort of boundary and definition. Who am I? How did I get here? Where am I going? The perennial existential questions enunciated by Sartre and friends[3] bother our days and disturb our sleep. There must be some focus, direction, sense of integrity.

The Focus and Integrity of Culture Is Maintained by the Stories We Tell

What a feeble foundation for the integrity of culture: stories. We all know that stories are not to be trusted, never have the truth, and certainly play fast and lose with the facts. True, and yet these apparent figments of our idle conversation perform a monumental task. Were it not so, would we ask, "What's the story?" upon entry into some new and strange culture, as in our first day on a new job?

After the employee orientation, after reading and being totally confused by the Employee Handbook, after the formal introduction to the arcane art of living in the new environment, do we not search out some apparently trustworthy soul to whom we plaintively address the most important question, "What's the real story?" And if we are lucky, he or she tells us . . . stories. How it all began, what happened last week, the "skinny" on the boss. The latest disaster. The Big Dream. Nothing but stories. And we don't even really care whether they are true or not—its just nice to know the Story. Somehow, it makes you feel at home. When you know the Story and are part of the Story, you belong. And if you don't know the Story, and are not part of the Story, you hardly even exist. So what is the story about Story? The Story is the organizational mythology.

But how can that be? There is nary a word about Zeus, Athena, and all the pantheon of Gods and Goddesses. The Story is just a story about everyday life—occasionally embellished.

All myths started life as simple stories of the everyday, and then they grew. The fact of the matter is, all myths are stories, although not all stories are myths.

The use of the word myth here, or anywhere, in standard conversation in the Western world, is sufficient to raise all sorts of red flags. We know that stories are not to be trusted, therefore we want the facts. But myth is absolutely beyond the pale. Worse than trivial, it is an outright lie. Or so we have all been taught.

In actual fact, myth is never true, indeed it goes beyond truth. The function of myth is to create the context in which the truth may be perceived as the truth. Double-talk, double-think? Maybe, but is this not our experience with the Story in any organization of which we have been a part?

For example, if the Story (or at least one element of it) is that the CEO's assessment of her organization and its inhabitants is neatly caught in a brief aphorism, "Never turn the asylum over to the inmates,"[4] do we have any difficulty in understanding why employees are treated with something less than full respect? Is it difficult to comprehend why innovation and accountability are in short supply? And do we have any problem in ascertaining the lack of truth of the annual dictum from the same CEO to the effect that we are all one big family? After all, we know the *real* Story. As we said, myth creates the context in which we determine the truth. Given a discrepancy between a statement by the CEO and the organizational mythology, there is no contest.

Myth wins every time.

Obviously every organization has a plethora of stories, so how does one, or a small group, become elevated to the exalted status of mythology? Quite simply, such stories are chosen, but not by committee, nor by the executive staff, and still less by the CEO. The process of choice occurs quite organically, and the choosing body is the whole organization, or perhaps we might say, the collective consciousness. Over time, certain stories just seem to "fit" in those critical situations when organizational definition is an issue. For example, in moments of crisis, when our organization must be defined in opposition to "them," some story from the past or present comes to the fore as a way of rallying the troops. The process continues in less critical situations, as when a new employee, tired of the official jargon, asks the important question, "What's the Story?" Given a little time, a core group of stories emerge as definitive, and in that moment, story becomes myth.

Myth Manifests Spirit in Time and Space The power of myth may be seen in many ways, as for example when myth and the CEO square off, figuratively speaking. As we saw, the CEO hardly even gets into the ring. But the fundamental power of myth arises from the fact that myth manifests Spirit in time and space.

The power to manifest Spirit is uniquely present in myth, but it is a power shared with any story. A good story becomes such not because it has assembled every possible fact and argument, for stories are usually brief, the facts questionable, and the argument thin to nonexistent. A good story creates a nutrient open space into which your imagination may flow to commingle with the imagination of the storyteller. And in the process, the essence of the tale comes forth. Or as we say, we get hooked.

The archetypical form of all storytelling is the circle, and most of us, usually in our youth, sat in that magic circle. Perhaps it was in Boy or Girl Scouts, at a family reunion, or on a camping trip, but somewhere along the line we sat by the campfire, imagined or real, to hear the tale told.

If it was a ghost story, we did not "get into it" by way of a long history of the diaphanous critters, or a closely reasoned scientific presentation. The ghosts showed up in the silences, feeding on the little scary details thrown to our imagination—a funny noise, a change in voice, and long significant pauses. Well done, the tale quickly turned from a "story about ghosts" into a real live encounter, which we would carry in our dreams from that night on—until we got too old for such things. In a word, Spirit showed up, albeit a ghostly Spirit.

We might also note that stories have a peculiar way of creating their own time and space, an ability demonstrated to each of us on those occasions when we find ourselves deep into a good book. Somehow we just get lost until our significant other, or maybe the cat, brings us back to current reality. With words or a meow it is pointed out that the night is well past, and what are we doing? The standard response is something like, "I just forgot what time it was."

Truthfully, that is a lie. We knew exactly what time it was. Ten-thirty in the morning of October 23, 1865 and we and our party are about to set out. . . . Once again the story had woven its own magic, and we have found ourselves in a very different time and space.

What is true for all good stories is especially true of myth. When the tale is well told, Spirit shows up. Not just the facts and figures, dead history, but the real live thing. Religious institutions have understood this very well, and go to great lengths to ensure that the story is well told. Their efforts are not always successful, but there is no doubting the intention.

Military units do much the same thing. The so called Unit History is not a dry recitation of the facts (if it is any good). It is a Spirit-churning experience through which the young recruits can feel the blood and sacrifice, the courage and determination of those who went before.

And please note: here are the core values, not presented in some dry abstract value statement, but in glorious living Technicolor. You can *feel* them, and with that feeling comes the possibility of organizational integrity at the deepest levels. Folks that feel together, stay together. Sure there may be arguments and disagreements, but all within a common context. We have a sense of oneness.

Myth manifests Spirit in time and space. It has always been so, and remains true even, and most especially, in those strange things called modern organizations. It was largely overlooked and often discredited in the days of the ProActive Organization, for after all we couldn't get involved with all that funny myth and Spirit stuff. It might get out of control. But the InterActive Organization is a different creature. Gone are the concrete boundaries and certainties of command and control, and in their place we must look for stronger, deeper forces to keep the organism intact. Culture is the medium, and myth the means.

TIME TO TELL THE TALE

If you have followed along to this point, you are doubtless ready to leave the world of abstract theory. It is time to tell the tale. To make all this real, allow me to tell the tale (mythology) of one of my clients. It is not elaborate; and indeed it consists of only four short stories. As I tell them, see if you can feel the Spirit of the place. Ask yourself, would I like to work in a place like that? Can I perceive its fundamental integrity and identify what is held to be good and true—otherwise known as values?

My experience with this client is now a number of years old, and I cannot swear that the stories I tell are still the ones of significance today. But at the time I worked with these people, the core stories were everywhere present at all levels and sectors of the organization, from the president to the shop floor. I should also tell you that there is a definite methodology for gathering these stories, which you may find described in the Appendix. Needless to say, you can't simply walk in and say, Tell me your mythology.

The Story of Jonathan

The Jonathan Corporation was a shipyard, and their major client was the U.S. Navy. Located in Norfolk, Virginia, with facilities in several other places around the country, they were definitely "the new kid on the block." Brash, young, and terribly good, they had some very new ideas about doing a very old business. The origin of their name, Jonathan, gives a quick indication of how they thought about themselves, for it came from the book, *Jonathan Livingston Seagull*.[5] Jonathan, the bird, was a daredevil creature, going where no seagull had ever gone before, pushing the envelope, with or without the approval of his parents and peers. Jonathan the company saw itself in similar terms, and their informal corporate motto was, "We Teach Engineers to Fly." Just imagine crusty old marine engineers taking off in very new directions.

Their name and self-image was not all hype. At the time that I worked with them they had never brought a job in late, or over budget. This record is remarkable in any business, and particularly so in the shipyard business where things tended to stretch on, and on, and . . .

So here is the story of Jonathan. See if you can catch the Spirit. I will tell each story briefly, and as I do, listen as you might to any story. Don't worry too much about the facts and figures, for they are few and far between, and put your analytical faculties on hold. Just get the flavor. If you feel like it, read the stories out loud. The printed page can be quite flat.

The USS *Speer* The *Speer* was a minesweeper sent to New Orleans over Mardi Gras for the pleasant duty of showing the flag during that wonderful celebration. On the way back down the Mississippi to the Gulf of Mexico, the captain apparently had too much Spirit of the wrong sort, and found himself looking at two totally unacceptable choices. Caught between a sand bar and an oil tanker, he had nowhere else to go. For reasons best known to himself, he chose the tanker, and the tanker claimed no small amount of the *Speer's* back end. With the damage done, the *Speer* limped home to the naval shipyard in Norfolk.

The Navy took a look and said that was a $3 million boo-boo, and put the job out to bid. Jonathan rose to the bait and ended as low bidder for $915,000. The Navy said Jonathan was crazy and looked at the numbers again, but concluded that the numbers added up, so Jonathan got the job—crazy as they were. It was their first big contract.

It was Christmas time and miserably cold. Freezing rain covered the ship, and most everybody from the president on down was out in the mess, welding and moving steel. Only a secretary remained in the warm office, and her job was to order up supplies as they were needed. And so it went, but the reward was sweet. They brought that sucker in three days ahead of schedule for $913,000.

Norma's Apartment Norma was a secretary, and one day fire swept through her apartment, leaving her with nothing. Within 48 hours, with no prodding from anyone, the good folks of Jonathan rallied 'round to provide Norma all things necessary to set up housekeeping once more.

The International House of Pancakes (The International House of Pancakes is sort of a McDonalds with a menu limited to pancakes.) In the early days of Jonathan, actually before it was officially organized, Gary Bowers, the soon-to-be president, and his close associate would meet there. They arrived with a pocket full of dimes (ten cent pieces), half of which were for the coffee, and the remainder for the pay phone outside, which was the corporate switchboard.

Phoenix Marine When Jonathan was scarcely one year old, several of the senior executives decided to try the business on their own. So down the street they went and opened Phoenix Marine in direct competition with Jonathan. On the day of their departure, Gary Bowers assembled his folks on the shop floor. He said, "As most of you already know, several of our people have chosen to go on their own. Should any of you care to join them, please be my guest. But if you choose to stay, there are two things you need to know. First, I respect these people as engineers and I respect their choice to go on their own. Secondly, we will compete with Phoenix Marine, eyeball to eyeball, no quarter given."

That's the Story of Jonathan. Out of all the stories that percolated through that shipyard, these were the ones that bubbled to the top. No matter where you went, or who you talked to, sooner or later you would hear about the *Speer*, Norma, the International House of Pancakes, and Phoenix Marine.

So how did it feel? How would you characterize the Spirit of the place? If you are like most people to whom I have told these tales, words like exciting, challenging, compassionate, rigorous, respectful, caring, frugal, no-frills, and competitive come to mind. Would you like to work in a place like that? And on the subject of values, do you have any problem identifying what the people of Jonathan held to be meaningful and important?

MYTH AT WORK

How does it all work? To get the picture, we need a picture, so just imagine that the field of meaning, the culture of Jonathan, is like a drum head, a big kettle drum head (see below). Each of the several stories are arranged around the edge in the position of the tuning handles. With that picture in mind, note that the effect of each story is not linear, but rather tensional (dialectic), and that collectively the stories create the resonant surface which produces the "sound" of Jonathan. Should any one of the stories lose its hold, so to speak, the sound quickly goes flat.

To see how this works, consider what would happen to Jonathan if the

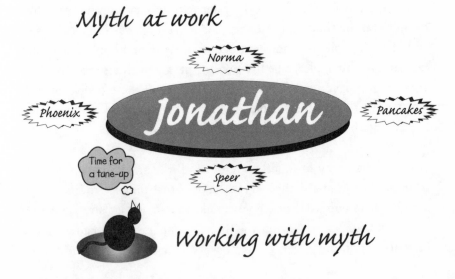

only story present were the *Speer*. To be sure this is a great story of competitive zeal, but if it were the only story around, the place would quickly turn into a sweatshop, characterized by stress, burnout, and worse.

Then, to turn things around a bit, imagine that the only story was Norma's Apartment. In a short space of time, this lean, mean, business machine would turn into a welfare state. Everybody would be so busy caring for everybody else that no useful work would get done.

A healthy Jonathan, an integrated Jonathan, a Jonathan with real integrity of Spirit comes into being only when both stories are present and effective. This is clearly another example of *both/and*, as opposed to *either/or*. Challenge must be balanced by compassion, and vice versa.

Think back for a minute and recall when we previously ran into such a polarity. Remember? It was all about Love. Love has two faces, challenge and acceptance, and we might also say compassion. It is not the word "love" that matters, indeed in Jonathan, the word never shows up, but the reality does, and that reality is critical to the health of any organization.

It has been noteworthy to me over the years, that all strong organizations, and Jonathan was certainly a strong organization, manifest the two faces of love somewhere in their mythology. If one side or the other is weak or missing it is a certain indication that at present or sometime soon, there is or will be real difficulty. When acceptance takes over, hard decisions are not made, and the fine edge of competence disappears. Should the challenge face of love dominate, the quality of organizational life quickly degenerates into a maelstrom of stress, anxiety, and burnout.

Working With Myth

Now that we have a working knowledge of the function of myth, it is time to put that knowledge to work. Let's suppose that you are part of the Jonathan crew, and suddenly there is a new, most important piece of work coming into the yard. It is a big job, and it must be done quickly and well, but conditions are anything but optimal. A lot of the guys have caught a nasty flu bug, and the weather is just abominable. Rain, snow, sleet, slush—but the job has to be done. So what story are you going to tell?

The *Speer*, of course! If all the fellows can catch something of the Spirit of those early days, what looks impossible might just happen. But how do you tell the story? Remember, this is a shipyard, so a glossy four-color brochure probably won't do it, and besides, it would take too long to get it ready.

Alternatives? Well, you might start with t-shirts—something like "Get Yourself a Piece of the *Speer*," given to those who demonstrate the right stuff. But that is just a start, and very soon you will have to call upon the storytellers, not to be confused with the corporate historian. Storytellers can make the tale come alive in language that everybody can understand. Typically you will not have to look too far, but the front office would not be the place to start.

At Jonathan, I happened to return for a visit sometime after my formal work with them had concluded. It was around Christmas time, and the weather was appalling. And guess what, they had a new big job sitting at the dock. Because Jonathan had been growing quite rapidly, there were a lot of new employees, folks who had not been there in the early days. They were doing the job, but not all that happily. During a break, a bunch of them had gathered under shelter to warm themselves. Conversation, such as it was, was pretty depressing. One gripe after another. The pay was wrong, the hours were long, and the benefits nowhere near compensatory. Each gripe led to another gripe in a downward spiral of shared misery.

Off to one side stood an old-timer. Kiley by name, he referred to himself as a "runty Irishman," which he certainly was, but he was much, much more. A master welder, well past the age of retirement, he came to work because he loved it, and when he lit his torch, it was clearly an artist working.

Kiley's arms were folded across his chest as he quietly watched the scene. And then you know exactly what he said, "Ah, you should have been there in the days of the *Speer* . . ." He said just enough to get the story started, with plenty of open spaces for the few other old-timers to add some details. In something less than 15 minutes the dismal atmosphere changed dramatically. Those who had been there told the tale, and the new folks hung on every word.

When the break was over and folks went back to work, it was a very different situation. Misery became challenge, and the wretched weather background detail for the next iteration of the story. But in the moment, the story had been told, and everybody was becoming part of that story—no longer just words, but common action.

I can't prove it, but I strongly suspect that nothing else could have produced the same results. And surely, answering each gripe in detail would have fallen far short. No amount of money, shortening of hours, or increase of benefits could possibly have had the same effect. When people hear the story, become part of the story to the point that the story is them, Spirit tends to soar and all the rest is just icing on the cake.

MYTH: THE DNA OF ORGANIZATIONS

Myth is serious business, and although it sounds quite commonplace, and works in remarkably simple ways, the effect is profound. At one level, working with myth is clearly not rocket science. At another level, particularly if we were to get into all the fine academic detail, the picture gets considerably more complex. However, at a working level, much of the detail just gets in the way. We, *Homo sapiens*, are fundamentally storytellers. It comes quite naturally, indeed it seems to be a part of our nature. But—and this is a huge BUT—to equate the simple and the natural with the trivial and inconsequential is disastrous. From where I sit, myth is to an organization what DNA is to an organism.

Just consider the amount of information coded into four apparently very simple stories in the case of Jonathan. To hear these tales, or more accurately to find ourselves in the midst of the complex fabric (field) of meaning created by their interaction, brings us face to face with the core values of the organization and the way in which they manifest in time and space. The experience is not just of intellectual knowledge, facts, or propositional truth, but something much more immanent, juicy, and alive.

All analogies fail at some point, but I have found the analogy of myth and DNA a useful one. Just as DNA encapsulates in an incredibly small space the necessary "instructions" for an organism's growth and development, so also does myth. And as we are learning, the individual genes, although simple off/on switches, never work alone, but always in combinations, even as the discrete myths themselves function interactively.

Making the analogy between DNA and myth is not my idea alone. Starting from the other end of the stick, as it were, biologist Richard Dawkins seems to be heading in a similar direction with his notion of "memes." For Dawkins, memes are the agents of cultural transmission, and "cultural transmission is analogous to genetic transmission." To be sure, meme and myth never show up in the same sentence, and Dawkins' idea of the meme is considerably less specific than my description of myth. For him, examples of memes include tunes, ideas, catchphrases, clothes and fashions, and ways of making pots and building arches.[6] But if he understood myth as I understand myth, I would like to believe that he would see the connection.

With or without Dawkins, I think the analogy holds, and to the extent that it does, messing about with myth is very serious business. Just as genetic engineering can substantially, and permanently, alter the nature of an organism, so "mythic engineering" might have a similar effect on organizations.

Mythic engineering (and I am not very happy with the words) is more than a theoretical possibility. Indeed I suggest that it is an essential skill for those who choose to live intentionally in the InterActive Organization, and particularly those who accept responsibility for its care and feeding. In an environment now understood to be fully open and constantly engaged with its surroundings, and where command and control are no longer operative, maintaining organizational integrity requires a deep understanding of the fundamental mechanisms that support integrity. And should the elemental integrity of the organization be challenged and/or corrupted, we will need to know how to restore wholeness and health. Suddenly myth moves from the level of trivial curiosity to that of a primary concern, and skill in the art of myth-making (mythic engineering) becomes a critical one.

With Jonathan we had a very healthy organization, and its mythic structure (DNA) both reflected that fact and created it. Not all organizations are so lucky. Consider the case of the Fortune 500 corporation mentioned above. The Story (at least one of the stories) was, "Never turn the asylum over to the inmates." With a basic myth like that, no amount of empowerment training, community building, or creativity enhancement programs would do much good. Indeed, there is a strong likelihood that all such courses and programs would be counter-productive. It is very difficult to feel empowered when the Story is that you are a bloody lunatic. In similar fashion, creativity and community quickly fall prey to the acids of such negative mythology. We need a new story.

chapter 12
Healing a Broken Spirit

JONATHAN WAS A STRONG ORGANIZATION, as reflected by the bottom line of its balance sheet, its reputation in the business, and the power of the stories it told. But not all organizations are so fortunate. Consider the corporation whose CEO thought in terms of asylums and inmates when speaking of her business and employees. The fact that she would do such a thing is questionable. The fact that her comment became part of the organizational mythology is disastrous, the cause and effect of a broken Spirit.

Interestingly enough, the corporation in question had a very healthy bottom line. In fact it was making money hand over fist. At the same time, the corporate reputation for being well managed was among the best in the country. Everything looked wonderful on the surface, until a fateful day when a corporate raider struck, and the organization was put to the test. At precisely the moment when spirited, to say nothing of inspired, performance was essential, it became clear to all that there was precious little in the gas tank.

The name of the corporation and the details of the struggle need not concern us here, for the situation they found themselves in is, unfortunately, by no means unique. Apparently successful organizations with strong bottom lines and good reputations will often have a nasty little secret. The Spirit is weak or broken and just hanging on. In the normal course of business, it doesn't seem to matter much, but come a crisis, and the truth will out.

When the flagging quality of Spirit, as reflected by a mythology composed of sad stories, begins to drag an organization down, the obvious solution is to tell a new story. But that is easier said than done, for the situation requires a new way of being, which precedes the storytelling. Thus, a new experience is a necessary precondition for the emergence of a new tale.

This piece of intelligence precludes a number of possible strategies. For example, obtaining the services of a corporate image maker will have limited impact. A new logo or motto may look smashing on the corporate stationery, but will do little for a troubled Spirit. Folks will ask, "Why do we look so good when we feel so bad?" The same may be said for changing advertising agencies, a full-blown internal campaign directed by Corporate Communications, motivational speakers, and programs for community building and personal empowerment. Good ideas, but not sufficient. At the end of the day, it all looks good, but feels pretty bad. Even the best efforts often produce little more than a momentary high followed by the crushing realities of "Monday morning."

TRUTH TIME

There comes a time when nothing but the truth will do. And it is not so much about telling the truth as about letting the truth emerge. For that emergence, a little Open Space is required. Open Space Technology is not a magic bullet, nor the answer for everything, but when the very life of an organization is at stake, the technique can be more than helpful.

Organizations, like all organisms in nature, are their own best healers. The central power for healing is the organization's innate capacity for self-organization. As we have seen, in nature this process enables the reformation (transformation) of the structures of living so that they may more appropriately address the challenges of the environment. It would be wonderful if we possessed the rational capacity to identify all the operative forces in the environment at large and within the organization itself, bring them into synergistic alignment, and accomplish the healing ourselves. However, the butterfly continues to land and the inherent complexities overwhelm. Fortunately, the process of self-organization works quite well without our assistance. But we can help.

Help can come in many packages, but one that I have found to be most effective works as follows. Begin with the stories of the organization, which you may gather by using the interview approach outlined in the Appendix. This will not take very long, as there is no need to talk to everybody in the place. A small number will do, usually no more than 20, provided you have been careful to select a true random, but nevertheless across-the-board sample—from the executive suite to the loading dock, so to speak. In short order, I believe you will find the operative mythology just leaping from the pages of your notes. Don't worry about their historical truth, for even if they never happened, or never happened in the manner described, it is only important that they are told as the common view of how things are around the workplace.

Analysis will not take long either. The good, bad, and indifferent will be pretty obvious. But remember, your assessment of the tales is of little importance compared to what the people involved may think. After all, it is their organization and their stories.

To find out what they think, my approach has been to convene what I call *Storytelling Time*, tell them the stories, and check it out. Everybody who has been interviewed is invited, along with anybody else who cares about the organization. This could be quite a lot of people, and in some cases the whole organization.

Prior to the event, I create cartoons, one for each story, or more if needed. My promise to the group is that I will tell the stories as I heard them, warts and all. This is truth time. And since some of the stories may be a little colorful, to say nothing of pointed, a dose of humor will usually take the edge off, but not too much. I leave it to your imagination as to how one might represent the CEO and the asylum.

No sources are cited, nor is there any need. If you have done a good job collecting the stories, everybody will know them already, so there is no reason to reveal where they came from.

When the guests are assembled, the show begins. Budget permitting, I make up a book for each person, and also I find working from a screen (overhead projector or video) a real plus. Done well, the cartoons speak for themselves, but an introduction to explain something of the nature of myth and how the material was gathered, and segues between segments, keep things connected and moving.

And what happens? First, what doesn't happen? I have never had anybody walk out, and even senior executives who may end up on the wrong side of a cartoon seem to take it in stride. I do find it useful, however, to do a little briefing to eliminate surprises—but not to allow censorship of the material. If all of this is going to be effective, the truth must be on the table.

And the truth does come out. Just to make sure, I ask everybody if they have all heard the stories before. The question is not whether they like the stories, but whether they have heard them. I have never had anybody challenge me on this point, which is not too surprising, because the folks I ask are, after all, the ones who told me the stories in the first place.

The impact of storytelling time is palpable. All of a sudden everything that everybody was whispering behind closed doors is right out there on the table. The pretense is over, and the sense of relief apparent. But the end is not yet.

As soon as the stories are told and validated, we move quickly into an Open Space event. The words of introduction usually go something like, "If I have just told the stories as you have known them, what is the story you would like to tell? What are the issues and opportunities for creating a business you would really like to be a part of?"

This may sound like a fast change of subjects, and it is. We are not convening an editorial committee to wordsmith the old stories to death. Rather we are inviting all present to talk about what has real heart and meaning for them, and then to get on with the most important business of making all that real. When the space is opened, the magic of self-organization takes over as the group collectively searches for new ways of being together. Rather than telling a new story, they *become* a new story.

Does it always work? Well it has to this point, and it probably continue to work so long as the truth is faced (the real Story is told), the space is truly open for people to explore what has deep meaning ı each and all of them. But the key is never to become attached to a prε determined outcome, even the outcome of organizational survival. I may be that the time has come to lower the curtain on that particular organizational life form. When it is over, it is over.

There was, for example, a small (50-person) consulting group that engaged in this exercise. By 1 p.m. they had determined that as an organization, they had no future. For the rest of their time together they imagined good and useful things that they might do in alternative configurations. And by the time they left, these new organizations were well on the way to reality. Explaining all of this to the Board and shareholders was a little difficult, but surely it was better to cut the losses and run than to allow things to dribble on to an inglorious conclusion.

KEEPING THE TRUTH ON THE TABLE: THE DEAD MOOSE SOCIETY

Facing the truth, and most especially unpleasant truth, is never easy. Something in each of us would rather look the other way, or never look at all. There is no reason to believe that things will be substantially different in the InterActive Organization. A Dead Moose Society can help.

As northern Americans know, and the rest of the world can imagine, a dead moose is large and smelly. When such a creature ends up beneath the organizational table, the results are not pleasant. People tend to keep their distance and nobody wants the nasty task of removing the critter. Sick stories (myths) are not unlike dead moose. Everybody knows they are present, and nobody wants to touch.

Storytelling time in Open Space has the capacity to identify the dead moose and start the process of removal, but a decent funeral is very much in order. Birgitt Bolton, a colleague in Canada (home of many moose), has developed an effective approach, which she calls the Dead Moose Society.

will
nd
r

ty convenes at the end of an Open Space, particularly when
dead moose have been uncovered. The venue for the meet-
lly a pub, which is probably not essential, but a few pints
ccasion along. The agenda is simplicity itself and centers on
il the stories of the deceased moose until none are left to tell, at
point the members feel complete and ready to let go and move
The stories usually start out with a very serious tone, but with the
passage of time and not a few pints, solemnity almost inevitably turns
to ribald humor. And when the laughter starts, the dead moose is definitely on its way out. Why people would ever want to hold on to a dead
moose is a mystery, but it seems to happen to all of us occasionally. The
therapeutic power of laughter is more than sufficient to send the creature on its way.

chapter 13
Everyday Life in the InterActive Organization

To THIS POINT, we have considered some of the basic and essential mechanisms for the maintenance of organizational integrity both at the level of information and knowledge flow necessary for collaborative effort, and at the deeper level of core values. It now remains to deal briefly with what we might call everyday life in the InterActive Organization. Doubtless as our experience increases with our new organizational lifeform, there will be more to say on the subject, but for the moment, three items of pertinence present themselves:

1. Take care of the "givens"
2. Tell the Story
3. Keep grief working

TAKE CARE OF THE "GIVENS"

The "givens" is shorthand for all those things that the organization just has to do. This is not about pursuing new passions, opening more space, indulging ourselves in High Learning—it is just taking care of business. What's got to get done.

I believe we are in for a pleasant surprise in this department, for an awful lot of what we used to think would fill our days just doesn't need to get done any more. Or if it does need to be done, it will not take as long. For example, the whole business of getting things organized used to consume endless hours. But with the gift of self-organization, that major task pretty much takes care of itself. Of course there will always be some things to tidy up, as it were, but the heavy lifting is pretty complete.

Nevertheless, there remains an irreducible list of must-dos, the givens. These include such things as making sure that people are paid, that the taxes are in on time, that the roof doesn't leak. To ensure that all of this will be taken care of, it will be useful to make a careful list. When we do, I think we will be surprised.

Most people I talk to assume that the list of the givens is an infinite one. After all, just think of all the things we *have to do*. But when we sit down and actually make such a list, it turns out to be a lot shorter than we expected, provided we ask a simple question every time we add an item to the list: "Do we really have to do it?" Is there some law, regulation, overwhelming social necessity that makes noncompliance unthinkable?

Several years ago, The U.S. Forest Service felt themselves to be overwhelmed with bureaucratic requirements. So much so that they were spending more time running the bureaucracy than doing the job they came to do, which was to take care of the forests, the creatures that live in them, and the people who visit. So they did a little study. It turned out that something like 85 percent of the "required" activities had been mandated at the level of the Service. The remaining 15 percent were congressional mandates, otherwise known as the law.

Concretely this meant that 85 percent of the identified givens were under Forest Service control. Doubtless, some of these regulations were very good ideas, but it was a matter of choice. When the people looked a little closer they discovered that more often than not some "given" was put in place in 1920 for reasons now lost in the mists of history. A very good idea at the time, but by no means necessary at the moment.

The chief of the Forest Service was Dale Robertson, who took a most courageous stand. He said to his troops, "If you find any regulation standing between you and the accomplishment of your job [which was neatly defined by the unofficial motto of the Forest Service "Care for the Land and Serve the People"]—*don't do it*. Should we run into problems we will deal with them, and if there aren't any problems we know that one more regulation (given) can come off the list."

I am sorry to say that Dale's courageous step was short-lived, compromised by a number of factors, political and otherwise, but he was clearly heading in the right direction. But another organization took up the challenge.

Wesley Urban Ministry was a small social service organization in Hamilton, Ontario (Canada). Their clients were the dispossessed of the earth: homeless people, battered women, recent immigrants. The executive director was Birgitt Bolton (to whom I owe a debt of thanks for the term, "given"), and she found herself in a position roughly equivalent to Robertson's. But she carried the process somewhat farther.

Like Robertson, she and her staff made a careful list of the givens. For reasons I do not know, the staff worked in two parts. The senior staff identified 12 things considered to be inescapable duties, and the balance of the staff named 52. I am not sure that I have the numbers precisely correct, and I do not know what the givens were in specifics. However, the difference between 12 and 52 yields some very interesting information. Forty of the givens were self-inflicted wounds. Further work on the part of everybody reduced the list to something like 6. All the rest was open space, to be dealt with as seemed most appropriate by the people on the job.

At this point, Birgitt and her people asked a brilliant question. *What is the minimum level of formal structure required to take care of the identified givens?* Upon close inspection, it turned out that the identified givens dealt basically with the external relations of the organization in two areas. There was a need to deal with the larger community and the press, and also a need to deal with the funds and funding of the organization, such things as banks, government, foundations. So the answer to the question about minimum necessary formal structure was two. There needed to be a CEO whose job was to interface with the community at large. There also needed to be a CFO to deal with the banks.

Wesley Urban Ministries did not stop with this intellectual exercise. They walked their talk and reduced their formal organizational structure to two positions with a minimal amount of supporting staff. Talk about flattening the organization! In one moment, the previous levels of bureaucracy were eliminated and everybody else suddenly had the opportunity to do what they had been trained for—deal with people. Supervisors to supervise the supervisors were ancient history. Essentially everybody was "on the line."

The impact on services delivered was remarkable. After a year of working with the new arrangement, it was discovered that the organization had doubled the services delivered/people served, for essentially the same level of budget. That is a whopping 100 percent increase in productivity. There were some other interesting effects, particularly in the area of employee retention. Turnover rate went down to just about zero, even though Wesley was paying its people somewhat less than comparable organizations in the area. The secret? People were doing what they really cared to do.

You might reasonably ask how they pulled all this off. Surely everything would have turned into a massive disorganized disaster. The real secret was that the people of Wesley, consciously and intentionally, sought to be what they called an Open Space Organization, or what I would prefer to call an InterActive Organization. Having enjoyed an Open Space event with the whole organization, they asked the reasonable question, why don't we do this every day? The conclusion was, why not? Staff meetings became mini open spaces, responses to community issues were handled in the way of Open Space. Given an issue, those who cared were invited to consider the possibilities and get on with the business. Just like that.

Considering that nobody I know of had ever quite done this before, Wesley was obviously walking into uncharted territory. There were problems and glitches, but it worked. Unfortunately the experiment was terminated when the board feared loss of its own power and the terrible possibility that things would get out of control. But those who were there on the working level saw productivity soar and Soul Pollution fall to record lows. Not too bad for a first effort.[1]

So how do you take care of the givens? Quite simply. First you have to figure out what they are. The list will be long at the start, but if you continue to ask—Do we really have to do that?—you will find that list shrinking before your eyes.

The next question is crucial: *What is the minimal level of formal structure necessary to take care of the identified givens.* In the days of the ProActive Organization, structure proliferated like a cancer. And like cancer it tended to kill things off, particularly if it was an arbitrary structure, arbitrarily imposed.

To be sure, there are some areas where our apparent need to structure things can be usefully applied, but the rule of thumb must be "less rather than more." And just to keep ourselves honest we might constantly be thinking of one more thing *not* to do. If it works all by itself, don't fix it.

This is all about gardening, and we need to become better gardeners, remembering that at the end of the day, the plants will grow all by themselves. Certainly we can establish the perimeter and erect certain structures to cut down on the passage of wildlife: deer, rabbits, and such. A little water will help, and gentle cultivation, but let the plants do their thing, and we will find that they do it very well. After all, they have had multiple millenniums for practice, and we are basically latecomers.

TELL THE STORY

To state the obvious, organizational integrity at the deepest levels is critical for sustained organizational performance. This is not about money, plant, facilities, or even technology, but rather core values. Certainly money is important, and you have to have a place to work and equipment to work with—even if the place is a virtual one, and the equipment no more substantial than bits and bytes floating in an electronic sea. But unless there is a clear and deep sense of who we are, what we are doing, and how we treat each other, all the rest is not that important. Answers to those crucial questions come from the Story, the mythology, the DNA of organization.

Organizational integrity, over the long haul, depends on three things: knowing the Story, telling the Story, caring for the Story.

Knowing the Story Is Everybody's Business

Knowing the Story is not simply a matter of being able to repeat the words, for by definition all members of the organization will be able to do that. After all, it is their organization and their story, and even if they do not know the precise details, they have the story in outline. But for most people most of the time, the full power and shape of the Story will remain outside of their critical awareness, as it probably should. After all, we get along quite well on a day-to-day basis with little if any critical awareness of our DNA. But that doesn't change the basic truth: Knowing the Story is everybody's business.

Traditionally, the job of knowing the Story was reserved for a priestly caste, who spent a lifetime learning the sacred texts and seeking understanding of their precise meaning. No matter what you may think of priests in general, the job was an important one, requiring dedication and expertise.

Should we now install a High Priest in all our organizations? Probably not, but a CMO (Chief Myth Officer) might not be a bad idea. After all we would not turn over the financial responsibility to people who didn't care about numbers and couldn't add. We cannot be less careful with the organizational DNA. Whether or not we create the new office of the CMO, it is imperative that concerned, knowledgeable people take a continuing interest in the nature of the Story and its health. The tools of the trade have been briefly outlined above and they, along with the abundant experience from such disciplines as Anthropology, need to be applied with sensitivity. From where I sit, few assets, tangible or intangible, are of greater value than the organizational mythology.

The problem with priests historically, and possibly also with a new corporate officer with the curious title CMO, is that not only did they know the Story, but they thought they owned it. The Story was their private preserve and power. Every so often this priestly class had to be reminded that the story was theirs only in trust, which was what the Reformation in its various iterations was all about.

The problem with priests, however, is at least partially a problem with the people who, for whatever reason, abdicate their own responsibilities and turn the story business over to the one or the few. Knowing the Story is everybody's business, and the more this is realized the greater the strength of the organization.

There are very practical reasons involved. In the days of the Pro-Active Organization we could have had a single CMO who would simply tell everybody else what the Story was, even as the CEO dictated the mission and policy, while the CFO took care of the numbers. Managers, of course, took care of the details. The InterActive Organization is very different. As a self-organizing creature it will grow and move in response to a constantly changing environment. No single person or small group can comprehend the complexity of its development and certainly cannot predict it. Among other things, this means that individuals who may have been very much in a side eddy of organizational life suddenly find themselves front and center—on the growing edge, as it were. If they are not firmly rooted in the Story, connected to the essential DNA, they will find themselves without support and therefore fail. Or they will find it necessary to create their own story at which point they will be on their way and lost to the organization. Knowing the Story is everybody's business.

Telling the Story

Broad knowledge of the Story obviously requires that the Story be told. But "telling" is by no means a simple affair, indeed the verb to tell may be misleading, for it suggests that all the action is verbal. Somewhere along the line we came to the mistaken conclusion that knowledge is purely a function of words spoken or written. Knowledge can be communicated by words, but only partially and usually superficially. It has been said that something like 90 percent of all communication is nonverbal. I can't vouch for the accuracy of the number, but my experience certainly validates the thought. So if not words, what then? We must consider all possible means and opportunities to tell the tale.

The Chart of Accounts One of the most powerful "bearers of the tale," in any organization is the Chart of Accounts. If the CEO says that people are the most important asset, and the Chart of Accounts places people clearly in the liability column, we know without even thinking about it where the truth lies. And it is not with the CEO.

The Chart of Accounts is usually left to the folks with green eyeshades, but it is much too powerful for such neglect. Our accounts tell us what we value and how much. When the story is that people are liabilities, we are not terribly far from the notion of inmates in an asylum. That may be going a bit far, but you can see the drift.

If it is the intention to reduce people to "liabilities," then the Story is in good shape, but should we have something else in mind, a little creative accounting of a positive sort will be in order.

How about we set a value on the people? And then place that value on the asset side of the ledger. Doubtless some bleeding hearts would object that you can't really set a dollar value on people. The accountants would mumble something about the "generally accepted accounting practices," but in truth most organizations can, and do, set a value on their people, and accounting practices can be changed.

On the subject of valuing people, every corporation I know of can tell you within a few percentage points what it will cost to recruit a new person, how much it will cost to train them, and what the downside costs would be if they weren't present. It may be a little rough, but the organizational balance sheet has other rough numbers, which nobody seems to object to—for example, the item which appears on the asset side of things with the interesting name of "good will" or "good name." This is purely a fudge factor, which tries to put some numbers on that most intangible thing we call *reputation*.

Actually, it you want to determine accurately what the people of an organization are worth, simply ask yourself, what would be the market value if everybody left? Surely it would be worth something if it were sold off for parts and pieces, but without the people? The formula is very simple:

market value – non-people value = people value.

A simple fix: put the "people value" on the asset side, and then run all the people costs against it. Such things as training, benefits, and vacation would no longer be what an accountant friend of mine used to call "dangling costs," things with no assets to back them up. We do no less with equipment and buildings, which are listed as assets, against which we charge things like maintenance and replacement. Why not with people? It would surely make a better Story.

The Calendar If you look at your organizational calendar could you learn anything about the Story? Probably not, and that is a shame. Here is where the religious institutions of the world have done a very smart thing. They have used our record of time to tell their story. It is impossible to be in a Christian, Muslim, Buddhist, or Hindu region over the course of a year without learning the essentials of their story. In the West we note the passage of Christmas, Good Friday, Easter (birth of Jesus, death of Jesus, and resurrection of Jesus). Not the whole story, but certainly enough to get you started. For the believer, the scroll of time tells a much richer version of the story. Every day has something new to add, whether it be a saint's day or some other sacred occasion.

Every time you look at your calendar, the story is told once again, but it goes a lot deeper than that. It is not just "verbal telling," but rather that the believer's time becomes sacred time, or if you don't like that religious word, it becomes story time. It is an ongoing drama in which the believer is an active participant. So the story is told not only with words, but with actions as well. Talk about experiential learning!

Celebration An integral part of any religious calendar are the periods of celebration, those special times and occasions when some significant element of the story is highlighted. Everybody gets into the Spirit of things, as it were. As we seek ways to maintain the integrity of our organizations we could do worse than to use this subtle tool. And what does your organization celebrate? Does it have anything to do with your story? Do all members of your organization find these celebrations to be an opportunity for reflection and renewal of core values? If not, why not?

Many years ago I had a client who called me up with a strange request. He said, "My Christmas party is terrible, please come fix it." I wasn't quite sure what he meant, so I went down to see for myself. He was right. It had no power, no meaning, and at worst it was a drunken brawl, usually avoided by any sensible person. The fix had nothing to do with improved party favors and decorations. It went right back to first principles. A powerful celebration highlights something that people genuinely care about, and in the case of my client some 90 percent of his employees were Jewish.

Artifacts Stories told with words alone get pretty thin, especially for that large group of people who just don't "get" something until they can see it, hug it, or carry it around. Ask yourself, if you walked into your place of work, would you have a clue about what the Story was, just by looking?

In most cases, probably not. The entrance will have a security desk and possibly some artwork on the walls, chosen for its aesthetic value, and sometimes (especially recently) for its monetary value, as organizations have discovered that "fine art" can be an appreciating asset. But what about the significant events in the life of this organization? The successes, the failures, the moments of triumph, the points of turnaround and renewal. Can you see them, touch them, taste them, smell them . . . ?

Newport News Ship Building did it right, I think. In front of their corporate headquarters, which faced the harbor and also their shipyards, someone had placed the first ship they had ever made. To my eye it was an ugly little steel vessel, and certainly vastly different from the massive aircraft carriers under construction in the yards. It stood alone right at the edge of the walkways leading from the parking lots to the work sites. Each day, thousands of workers passed by, some giving this ancient artifact a friendly pat on the bow, so that over the years the paint had worn off and the raw steel showed through. Just in front and to one side of this little ship there was a bronze plaque with the corporate motto. It said, "We build good ships. At a profit if we can, at a loss if we must. We build good ships."

Wonderful! You could see it, hug it, taste it—even give it a pat—and that sensate experience was linked to one of the best statements of core values I have ever seen. Here was the Story displayed in ways that appealed to all the senses and also the mind. Anybody passing by could get a very good idea of where things started and why the journey was undertaken. Sad to say, when Newport News Ship Building was sold to some other corporation several years ago, I am told that the little ship and the corporate motto were removed. I guess the new owners didn't like the part about loss. They really didn't understand the Story.

Initiation When do you tell the Story? Anytime, any way you can. But there are special times in the life of an organization when telling the tale is not only important, but crucial. One of these times is at the point when new people join up.

In most organizations familiar to me, the introduction of a new member is marked by little more than a brief orientation in which benefits are explained and responsibilities outlined. Not a word about the Story, and if the Story is half as important as suggested, this omission is worse than stupid, it verges on criminal.

Doing an effective job at the point of entry is all about initiation. In addition to providing information about the practical details of life, introduction to the Story is essential, and a five-page pamphlet outlining the organization's history won't do the job. There are organizations that handle this task with excellence, and the military is right at the top of the list.

There is a special name for this introduction: boot camp. I am not suggesting that all organizations need to adopt the rigors of military life, but borrowing a few of the ideas would not hurt at all.

Boot camp is where you first learn to be a soldier, and the knowledge gained is only minimally cognitive. You march it, sweat it, do pushups over it, sleep it, eat it—and there are master storytellers in charge. They are called drill sergeants. All of the "techie stuff" comes later. Boot camp goes right to the soul of the matter, and it seems to take about six weeks to turn a raw recruit into something approaching a soldier.

Precisely what initiation should look like in your organization obviously depends on the nature of your organization and its story. Initiation in a social service institution will look vastly different than in a software firm, but the core elements will be similar. And it is all about the Story: how it all began, the triumphs and tragedies along the way, and just as important, the dreams of things to come.

Do not forget the tragedies, or what some might call failures. It is very tempting to put all of this aside, and dwell only on the successes. Indeed if we were to look only at the annual reports of American corporations (which supposedly tell the Story), it looks quite clear that none of them ever failed. And this failure to note failure carries a very high price tag. Not only does it give the false impression that everything is always rosy, which in turn engenders the futile expectation that it will always be so, but the end result is inevitable frustration and a sense of betrayal.

Gregory Bateson reminds us that what goes up will come down—sooner or later. And when it comes down, those who have been looking at the world through rose-tinted glasses will not only be surprised but will feel, understandably, that they weren't given the whole story.

Neglecting the tragedies and failures of the organizational story has another, and perhaps steeper cost. The newcomers will be denied the essential information about how the organization deals with adversity. The story of Phoenix Marine told at Jonathan is a wonderful example of what *should* be done. When a significant part of the senior leadership left, that was certainly a tragedy and might be considered a failure. But those who hear the tale will know that under similar circumstances, the first step is to acknowledge the situation straight on. No excuses, and certainly no belittlement of those who chose to go. And then get on with the business. As Gary Bowers said, "We will compete with them eyeball to eyeball—no quarter given."

And make it real! A printed version, even something as elegant as a well-produced video, will pale in comparison to literally walking in the steps of those who have gone before. If your organization were Jonathan, you would help the newcomers get a piece of the *Speer*. But not too cheaply, for that would cheapen the whole affair. Take them out, let them struggle, and then bring in the storytellers to interpret the total experience. In this department, the Kileys of the world should be considered an invaluable resource. Nobody—not the president, not the Director of Communications—nobody can tell that story like Kiley.

A Thousand Ways to Tell the Tale There are a thousand ways to tell the tale, and no one of them is perfect. As we learn the subtle powers of myth making and storytelling, our level of competence will improve. Experimentation, however, will remain a central activity, guided by a few simple principles. First, tell the whole story and don't gloss over the tragedies and failures. Second, keep it simple. There is no reason to lay on a full recitation of all the "facts," especially when the facts of the case are in short supply. Even if something never happened as described in the tale, or never happened at all, it is significant that the collective consciousness picked up the tale as descriptive of itself, and prescriptive of behaviors down the road. And third, make it real. Remember, most people just don't get words. While words are important, they are only a tiny part of the communicative spectrum. Don't forget about smell, touch, kinesthetic experience, sight (other than the printed page) and sound (other than the spoken word). In short, tell the story appropriately using the full range of communication—dance, drama, song, music, graphic arts, plastic arts. Don't overdo it, but don't be afraid to try things out. There are few things more critical to organizational health than a good story well told.

KEEP GRIEF WORKING

In the days of the ProActive Organization, preservation was accomplished by what we called "institutionalization." Once the form and function of the business had achieved a certain level of effectiveness, it was locked in place with institutionalized structures and procedures. The InterActive Organization is quite different, so much so that to institutionalize it is to essentially sign its death warrant. The sentence may be carried out sooner or later, but whenever the world changes again, the rigid institutional forms will lack sufficient flexibility to reconfigure themselves in order to meet the new challenges.

More to the point, the essence of the InterActive Organization lies in process and not structure. Structures may, and will, come and go with alarming rapidity, but as long as the core process is in good shape, all will be well.

The process, of course, is self-organization, which requires the essential preconditions common to all natural systems. In Stuart Kauffman's version, these precondition are:

▼ A relatively safe nutrient environment
▼ A high level of diversity
▼ Sparse prior connections
▼ A drive toward improvement
▼ Being on the edge of chaos

Given these preconditions, the process of self-organization will begin, as we have seen over and over again. Complex Adaptive Systems appear, structure happens, Order for Free.

However, the InterActive Organization is not just any natural system, it is specifically a human system, and as we have seen, human systems have a special way of negotiating the rigors of self-organization as they adapt to changing environments. It is called Griefwork.

The Griefwork process operates pretty well by itself. Given the appearance of chaos in our individual or collective lives, a predictable pattern comes into play. Shock/Anger, Denial, Memories, Despair, Open Space, Vision, and off we go. Or not. The process is apparently "hard-wired" into our essential humanity. It comes with the territory, so to speak. However, when the process is known and assisted along its way, the running time may be shorter, and the experience less traumatic. Very much like the process of birth, there is not much possibility of changing it, but knowledge of the steps and help along the way can be very useful.

Knowledge of the Process

When we suddenly find ourselves in the middle of grief with no fore-knowledge of what is going to happen, the experience can be terrifying. However, armed with such foreknowledge, the process is no less painful, but at least we know the steps along the way, and that it will end. It is even possible to make the process work for us, as I discovered a number of years ago in a curious situation.

I was writing my first book, *Spirit: Transformation and Development*, on my first computer, the venerable KayPro, operating under CPM—which places all of this very much in the days that the dinosaurs walked the earth. One day I was hot into the chapter on Griefwork in Organizations. Words and ideas were flying with no apparent effort, and after a number of hours, I put the final period in the final sentence of what I knew to be an outstanding piece of prose. And then . . .

Chaos struck, the power blinked off and on. My literary zeal had been such that I forgot the unforgettable: Save your material. And the wonderful auto-backup feature had yet to be invented. I just sat there like a "doofus" watching the computer go through its startup routine, ending as it used to in those days with a blank screen except for the little C:\>, the old DOS prompt. As for my chapter, it was all cyberhistory.

My first response was profane—"Oh _____! Then I thought it can't really be gone. Surely somewhere in all those files I will find the missing material. No such luck. And then I thought to remember what I had said . . . And just at that point, I started to laugh. Here I was writing about Griefwork, and going through the process myself. Shock/Anger, Denial, Memories . . . everything was appearing right on cue.

My knowledge of the process turned out to be very helpful. Instead of sitting there agonizing over each forgotten detail, and knowing that even though I might get the substance right, the essential flow would have vanished, I just let it all go. Shutting down the computer, I went out for a long walk, followed by a nice dinner and a good sleep. In the morning it was a new day and a new chapter rolled out. The memories of pain and frustration remained, but they were largely offset by the act of having created something new and possibly better.

So the first order of business when it comes to keeping Griefwork working is to make sure that all the people know the process. It is not complicated, and doubtless they have been through it before. When disaster, large or small, strikes again as it surely will, they will definitely have a leg up. How and when this precious piece of information should be communicated is a matter of choice, but a small section in the initiation program entitled *Survival Skills in the InterActive Organization* would be a good place to start. And it would not hurt to illustrate this presentation with copious references to those elements in the Story recording previous disasters. Of course, if all such disaster tales have been conveniently forgotten, the illustrative material will be pretty thin, and the Griefwork presentation too abstract to be useful.

Helping People through Griefwork

Griefwork is something that cannot be done for somebody else. No matter how much we might wish to shoulder the pain and protect our fellows, that is not possible. But we can help.

Help in this instance is very much like the sort of help that a midwife offers to a woman in labor. From the start it is clear that the woman bearing the child must travel the road herself. But the midwife offers two useful things: a knowledge of the twists and turns the road is likely to take, and a little company on the journey.

Even though we may know the Griefwork process intellectually, backwards and forwards, even though we have read all the books and attended every seminar, when everything hits the fan, it is awfully easy to forget. At such a time it is useful to have someone around who may not have been hit quite so badly, and who can sort of keep score as we go along, and help out with a few suggestions.

Sustaining the Griefwork process helps sustain the process of life itself in our organizations. Should that process cease, nothing else makes much difference. Of course there are no guarantees, even as there are no guarantees for the newborn. But the possibilities are clearly immense. I believe that just as this process is fundamental to the continuance of an organization, so also the nurturing of that process is the most important thing that any of us can do under the heading of the Care and Feeding of the InterActive Organization.

Given the importance of the process and the essential role that must be played in assisting its progress, it might be assumed that all of this is something best left to the experts. There is no question that expert opinion can be helpful, but being fully present as the process rolls is everybody's job. In the first place, there are not enough experts to go around, given the massive doses of chaos we experience as our environment changes and changes again. More fundamental, however is that being fully present with others in their moments of grief is a defining moment of our own humanity. At such a time we give and receive the most incredible gifts. Along the way we may just start to understand who we are and what we might become.

chapter 14

Ethics in the InterActive Organization

WHEN WE ADMIT CHAOS INTO POLITE SOCIETY and acknowledge that it has a useful function to play, much of what we used to consider bad and evil looks rather different. The simple dichotomy (order is good and chaos is evil) that defined much of our ethics in the ProActive Organization is no longer possible.

To see the point in the larger arena of the natural order, we need only remember the title of a recent book, *The Perfect Storm*.[1] The book describes a massive Northeast gale that churned the Atlantic off the Grand Banks, producing waves in excess of 100 feet and wreaking havoc on fishing fleets and mariners of all sorts. Life was lost, boats were sunk—and this was a "perfect storm?"

And yet from the storm's point of view, if I may be permitted the anthropomorphism, the storm was doing neither more nor less than it was supposed to do, perfectly. Violent natural events are most inconvenient for human beings if you happen to be in their way, but it is precisely these massive events, and their smaller relatives, which have enabled the living system, planet Earth, to become what it presently is—a hospitable place for us and all the other creatures. Just another day at work for chaos.

We may see the logic, but somehow it is repellent, especially when applied to the level of human activities. Adolf Hitler and the Third Reich, for example, obviously represented a massive outbreak of chaos in the ordered world of Western society. Clearly evil was present. Yes, but it may also be argued that from the point of view of world history, the chaos of the Third Reich was nothing more than the natural operations of a massive complex adaptive system (the Western world) engaging in the process of transformation.

Chaos in the form of Hitler created a lot of Open Space in which the new societal forms of the post-World War II era have emerged. Despite the obvious problems and difficulties of present-day life, few of us would like to return to a world dominated by colonial empires and characterized by the repression of subject races in places like India and Africa.

AN AMORAL UNIVERSE?

An easy way out of the dilemma is simply to eliminate the notions of good and evil. Things just are. With this view, morality has no place in the natural order, including our small part of the natural order. Storms are just storms, Hitler is just Hitler, and of course, business is just business. What happens, happens, and there is neither good nor bad.

Actually, such an amoral view is not terribly far from what a number of us have taken to be standard business practice. When a deal is done, a company sold or bought, we need not concern ourselves with anything but the bottom line. It is all about money. The fact that people lose jobs, families are disrupted, careers terminated, is glossed over with the convenient phrase: "It's just business."

Recently more than a few of us have registered some complaint with this way of looking at things. It is suggested that business should be concerned with more than the bottom line. Or that perhaps the bottom line should be recorded in ways other than, and in addition to, the financial return on investment. But at the end of the day, it seems that the dollar (pound, yen, mark) still rules.

I would agree that the simple equation of business and the financial bottom line is very short-sighted. But I would also point out that even in this hard-nosed approach there is a morality of sorts. Morality, after all, is all about values—what we care about. When money and other substantive concerns (buildings, automobiles, etc.) constitute what is valued, the bottom line, in hard cold cash, is very moral. So the real issue is not about money, or even values (as in do you have some?), but rather *what is it that is valued?*

ETHICS AND SPIRIT

With the advent of the InterActive Organization, the whole question of what is valued takes on a very different appearance, and as a consequence ethics and morality come out in vastly different ways. The Good (*summum bonum* as Aristotle would say) is no longer the forms and structures of our world and their concrete manifestations, but rather the integrity of the process of life itself. And the coin of the realm is no longer the toys we may have accumulated along the way, but rather the quality of Spirit manifest in the people and places of our existence. As our attention moves from substance to Spirit, some interesting things happen. There was a day when we might have jokingly said, "Whoever has the most toys wins." The joke may now have to be revised to something like, "Whoever has the most fun wins," for fun, after all, is a critical earmark of spirited enterprise.

This is not about altruism or spirituality, although both of these are probably quite useful. It is about simple common sense. As we have discovered, Spirit is the most important thing. When Spirit is fully present and working well, transforming in an ongoing search to more adequately fit its environment, good things happen. Organizations become exciting, alive, and profitable, if profit is a major concern. By the same token, when Spirit becomes flabby or out of focus, or is just plain gone, not very much gets done. And for sure, such toys as we have look pretty dull.

Ethics is caring for the most important thing, in this case Spirit. Ethics is not an endless list of "oughts and shoulds," but a practical set of requirements to assure proper caring. We know that Spirit does not respond well to arbitrary commands, although it is always open to invitation. We also know that iron-fisted control is a real Spirit killer, and therefore should be avoided. Arbitrary and inappropriate structure gets in the way and restricts the free flow of Spirit as it seeks new expressions of itself. The ethics of the InterActive Organization require the minimal formal structure necessary to get the job done. No more. No less.

These "requirements," and doubtless a number more, must be met, or Spirit leaves. Simple as that. There is no necessity to wait for some final judgment day, for judgment is rendered instantaneously and without partiality. Mistreat Spirit and everything falls apart. We may then be left with our toys, but they no longer interest us. The Spirit of play (playful Spirit) has simply vanished.

HAVE WE FINALLY GOTTEN RID OF EVIL?

It may have occurred to you as we have explored the emergence and nature of the InterActive Organization that we have finally gotten rid of evil, and/or that my enthusiasm has gotten the better of my judgment. I think that neither of these possibilities are true. There is no question that I am excited, indeed elated, by the emergence of what I take to be our new organizational lifeform. As I experience it in the natural laboratory of Open Space Technology, and increasingly in the world at large, I find huge optimism building for the realized potential of us all. For the doomsayers, who are sure that we are all going to hell immediately if not before, I say hold on, the reports of our imminent demise are premature. Clearly the world as we have known it is passing from view. This passage has been, and will continue to be painful, difficult, and quite often just plain terrifying. However, there is light at the end of the tunnel, sunrise after the darkness, and life after the ProActive Organization. We still may manage to scuttle good (space)ship Earth with massive doses of pollution, both environmental and of the soul. But that is not a foregone conclusion, so far as I am concerned. But have we gotten rid of evil? No.

Evil, along with all the rest of our experience, is transforming, or perhaps it is more accurate to say that our perception of evil is transforming. As we become more comfortable and aware of our life in the realm of Spirit, we will also become more aware of the subtle instruments affecting that realm. And with an increase of awareness should also come an increase in our skill in the use of such instruments, for good or evil. One of these instruments, and possibly the most powerful, is myth, the DNA of organization.

To fully appreciate this point we may recall the name of Hitler. We all remember who Adolf Hitler was and how he ended up. But we may not remember how it all began. In the early 1920s Hitler was considered little but a crazy fool, wandering the beer halls of Bavaria in the company of his cronies. Except that Hitler's father changed his own name in 1876, Adolf could have been known to history as Adolf Schicklegruber. Hardly a name to echo down the halls of history.

How quickly things changed. In 1933, the Reichstag burned, and that fire spread throughout Germany and on to the world at large. Considering how fast Hitler moved and how far his power extended, one might wonder what power he had to begin with. The answer is precious little. But he and his colleague, Goebbels, really knew how to tell a story. Building on the disaffection of the German people arising from any number of factors, including the stringent terms of the Versailles Treaty that concluded World War I, followed by the harsh economic realities of the Depression, Hitler tapped into the deep wellsprings of Teutonic mythology. Iron, Race, Steel, Blood were all orchestrated in the pageantry of Nuremberg, and all too soon Germany was on the march, goose-stepping across Europe.

In truth, Hitler had little but the power of story/myth on his side, but he used it well and with great skill. How much of this was conscious, I really can't say, and usually his activities in this area were cloaked in the apparently neutral term of "propaganda." But I would call it mythic engineering with a vengeance.

Hitler realized, in one way or another, what cultures from time immemorial knew very well, that sacred stories were extraordinarily powerful. Such power was traditionally guarded by a priestly group as a closely held secret, and one might argue that Hitler and his friends were the de facto priesthood of the Third Reich. The modern world—and yes the world of the 1930s was very much a part of the modern world—had turned a blind eye on the deep forces of myth and Spirit in the name of scientific rationalism. After all, such things were little but romantic superstition. But while so-called rational folks were looking the other way, Hitler worked his magic, albeit black magic. All the rest is history.

We can learn much from Hitler, mostly under the heading of things that must never be done again. But should we throw the baby out with the bath water we will miss a most important lesson. The diabolical results of Hitler's reign had their origin in deep power: the power of culture and myth in the realm of Spirit. To overlook, or deny, these powers is to turn it all over to the Hitlers of this world. And unfortunately there have been others, and doubtless there will be more. Like the power of the atom, we can use it for good or evil. The choice is ours. As I said, ethics are important.

During the time of the ProActive Organization, access to the subtle realm of myth was largely denied through our ignorance, which in turn bred trivialization of all things mythical. After all, myths were just idle stories, primitive superstitions, and definitely not to be taken seriously. With the exception of an elite few, including Hitler on the dark side, and probably the likes of Gandhi and maybe also Martin Luther King—both of whom understood the power of Story—myth was not something to be bothered with. And here is a case where ignorance truly was bliss. It kept us out of a lot of trouble. However, as ignorance passes to awareness and from thence to knowledge and skill, the possibilities are indeed unsettling.

Bombing cities and shooting people, even capturing all their toys, pale in comparison to the destructive possibilities of the misuse of myth. The former aberrations merely destroyed the externals. With myth it is possible to go right to the soul, and the diabolical possibilities are enormous.

So have we gotten rid of evil? No. If anything, we have merely raised the stakes. It is an ancient understanding, coded in the notion of yin and yang. Where there is light, there is also shadow, and the stronger the light, the deeper the shadow. We could of course hope for some shadowless existence, which would be very flat and utterly boring. Hardly a life worth living. For myself, I see no reason to pull the plug. The possibilities available to the human Spirit are truly awesome and the responsibilities are of equivalent magnitude. The journey should be quite a ride.

Epilogue

MY STORY IS DONE. And it ends pretty much as it began, with Spirit. For all those people whose Spirit may be tired, as well as all those other people who have responsibility for organizations and institutions in which the Spirit may be sagging—just remember, it really doesn't have to be this way. There are alternatives. Soul Pollution is not inevitable. And the cure is very simple: open some space, and Spirit will certainly show up. Allow the magic of self-organization to work for you, and the complex adaptive system that we are will find its own power.

If you find it personally difficult to open some space, just wait for the next influx of chaos. Don't resist it. Make chaos welcome, for space is being cleared so that creation and learning may take place.

And in that space you will find Spirit going on a journey of discovery. Old things will be put away, and new things will emerge. That journey will not be pain-free. It begins in shock and anger, but it ends (usually) in Vision. It is a journey each one of us must take by ourselves. It is also a journey we can help each other through. Like a midwife at the birth of a child, we may assist at the birthing of the new forms of Spirit.

Now—right now—is a very special time. Even though Spirit is always forming and transforming in ourselves and in our organizations, this is a moment of sea-change. The venerable ProActive Organization, which has served us well, seems to have run its course. The gifts of efficiency and massive productivity also have their price, which is now due. Environmental pollution and Soul Pollution make it quite clear that going forward as we have traveled in the past is to invite an unpleasant ending to the human adventure. Doing business as we have done business in the past is a sure prescription for going out of business—permanently.

But there is an alternative now coming into view. Seen from the point of view of the ProActive Organization, the newcomer appears counter-intuitive, impossible, or just plain wrong. Worse yet, it requires that we let go of the one thing we most dreaded losing: control. At least the sort of control we thought we had. But it is turning out that once we give up what was never ours to begin with, we may experience a remarkable renewal of our humanity, characterized by High Learning, High Play, appropriate structure and controls, and best of all, genuine community. Such are the gifts of the InterActive Organization.

It is indeed a strange and wonderful new world. Strange, because much of what we had previously thought to be the essential tools for the maintenance of organizational health either don't work or are counter-productive. It is wonderful because new ways are showing up for the proper care and feeding of the InterActive Organization. Naturally, we are not quite clear what we are doing as yet, but clues are definitely in the wind, possessing an almost charming simplicity: take care of the givens, tell the Story, and keep grief working.

This charming simplicity can be deceptive, for even though the level of our *doing* drops markedly, the quality of our *being* becomes that much more critical. In a word, our ethics and our values are no longer subjects of incidental concern to be dispensed with through the publication of a values statement. What used to be "nice" is now essential. And the reason is simple. The proper care and feeding of the Inter-Active Organization requires the use of elemental realities of immense power, such as myth. The potential for good is staggering. The potential for evil is equivalent. The responsible choice is ours.

My story is done, but our story will continue. We have much to learn and many joys and sorrows to experience. And someday, I am sure, what is new, strange, and exciting at the moment will be definitely an old story. At that point we will be ready for the next installment, the Inspired Organization. In the meantime, the journey goes on as Spirit continues to form and transform.

APPENDIX:
COLLECTING THE STORIES

The most accurate and efficient way to collect the stories of an organization is through a series of interviews with a random group from the organization. I sometimes call this a Noah's Ark sort: two of everything. The precise number does not make a lot of difference, and by the time 10 to 15 individuals have been interviewed, the tales have been essentially identified. Additional interviews are more a matter of confirmation and politics. Thus if one continues on through another 10 to 15 interviews and finds no substantial variation in the results, it is a safe bet that the story has been received. On the other hand, if major variations or additions appear, add interviews until the situation stabilizes. Deciding when enough is enough is always a judgment call, and while it may be possible to statistically validate the findings, I am not at all sure there is any added value. There comes a point when you hit the end of the road and it is pretty obvious.

My reference to *political* concerns refers to those individuals in an organization who just have to be interviewed. Thus, if there are two unions representing the workers of an organization, it simply will not do to interview only one of the local presidents. The same logic applies to senior vice presidents.

INTERVIEW FORMAT

The purpose of these interviews is not to gather facts and figures—hard data—but rather to provide a safe, supportive environment in which people may tell the tale. It is important that they tell the story in their own way, and therefore rigidly structured approaches will not work. From a methodological point of view, this approach is more like that of a field anthropologist operating as a participant observer than anything else. While there is no one right way, my practice is as follows.

I ask each subject to set aside an hour and a half. We almost always use all that time, and quite often more. If possible, I like to do the interviews on the subject's turf or in some neutral area. To be avoided like the plague is the practice of summoning all subjects to some central interview room.

At the commencement of the interview, I explain that my purpose is to gather the tales of the organization as a means of engaging the essential Spirit of the place. I may take a little longer than that to lay out the details, but there is never any question as to why I am interested. And I make it quite clear that should the subject, for any reason, feel uncomfortable and wish to terminate the interview, that is fine with me, and no questions will be asked.

Once I have a green light, the subject is informed that there are only two questions: what is this place, and what should it be?

Rarely is it necessary to define "this place," as context does the job quite well. It is also an interesting piece of information if the subject defines the boundaries of the establishment in unexpected terms, which suggests that the official version of the story (what we are doing around here) is at some, and possibly some considerable, variance with the story in the streets.

While my interviewee is contemplating answers, I propose an interim question as follows: "While you are thinking of your answers, it would be very helpful to me if you could share a bit about who you are, and how you came to be here." Obviously I am searching for a little biographical information, which will be useful for the interpretation of the tales as told. But I am also, and most importantly, providing the opportunity for the subjects to tell their own tales, an opportunity that few can resist.

In short order the conversation is completely centered on the subject, where he or she came from, how long ago, education, major happenings along the way to the future. As if by magic, the hour and a half allotted for the interview evaporates and never once do I return formally to the two questions I proposed at the outset: what is this place, and what should it be? The reason is a simple one. There is no need. As the individual's tale is told, there emerges simultaneously that person's perspective on the organization as a whole, the times of triumph and the times of trouble. The detail may be quite thin, covered only with words like, "I arrived just after the . . . and was it ever (exciting, awful, boring, stimulating)," but there is no question that you are listening to the echo of a defining moment in the life of the organization, the sort of stuff myths are made from.

PERCEIVING THE SPIRIT

One story, once told by a single person, does not a myth make, even if that person happens to be the CEO, chairman of the board, or managing director. Nor does a single telling lead inexorably to the soul of the organization. However, if you hear this tale told again and again as you go through the interviews, you can be certain that you are in the presence of the organizational mythology and close to perceiving the reality of Spirit. It is then only a matter of keeping score. How may times did you hear this tale and who told it?

As the several interviews progress and the defining moments are laid out on the table, an expanding picture of the organizational mythology makes itself apparent. What the people choose to mention as significant to their life in general, and in the organization, gradually assumes a pattern. Out of all of the possible moments of significance to the organization, certain ones have been retained in the collective memory. One may question their accuracy, indeed even their historicity, but one cannot question their presence in the mythology as a powerful and formative force for the Spirit of that place.

It is useful at this point to underline the difference between myth and history. With history we are concerned with the facts, nothing but the facts, so far as that is possible. Myth operates in a different sphere. Factual authenticity may exist or not, but that has little if anything to do with the power of a particular piece of mythology to shape and form the Spirit of a place. To complain that a certain myth is not true is to miss the point. For better or worse, good or bad, true or not, the myth is present. The only useful question is, what is the effect? How is Spirit imaged?

For example, if the organizational story is that management is only out for itself and concerned for its own well-being, while leaving the business, customers, and employees to look after themselves, it does not take a special intelligence to intuit the level, quality, and character of Spirit in that place. If it then turns out that some of the managers are the soul of generosity and compassion, they unfortunately will be seen through the spectacles of the myth as either frauds or wildly aberrant exceptions. For after all, the story is . . .

NOTES

Prologue

1. For a full account of Open Space and its applications, please see my books, *Open Space Technology: A User's Guide* and *Expanding Our Now: The Story of Open Space Technology*. Both are published by Berrett-Koehler (1997). The first book supplies the "how-to" and the second describes the history of Open Space Technology and offers some interpretation.

2. I am not sure that the case would be any stronger, but for sure my pride of creation would be enhanced, were I to have begun my adventure in Open Space with a consciously stated hypothesis, conditions, and procedures. Truthfully, I just stumbled into it. But that is the nature of a natural experiment, and probably says a great deal about the [f]utility of pride.

3. Our hesitancy could be, of course, because Open Space is an unknown, but such lack of knowledge cannot be due to a lack of exposure. Open Space has been described in detail in countless national and international publications, including the *New York Times*, the *Washington Post*, *Training Magazine*, the *ODN Practitioner*, the *Financial Times of London*, *Success Magazine*, and more.

4. Kauffman, Stuart. *At Home in the Universe*. Oxford: Oxford University Press, 1995.

Chapter 1: Chaos and the End of Control as We Knew It

1. Chandler, Alfred. *Strategy and Structure: Chapters in the History of American Industrial Enterprise*. Cambridge, MA: MIT Press, 1962.

2. Isaiah 45:7. The translation is mine.

3. Gleick, James. *Chaos: Making a New Science.* New York: Penguin Books, 1987.

4. For the full tour as described by an early practitioner of the arcane art of Chaos watching, see Ilya Prigogine's *Order Out of Chaos.* Toronto: Bantam New Age, 1984.

5. Gleick, James, *op cit.,* p. 298.

6. Bateson, Gregory. *Mind and Nature: A Necessary Unity.* Toronto: Bantam, 1980.

Chapter 2: Chaos and Learning

1. Mahesh, V.S. *Thresholds of Motivation.* New Delhi: Tata McGraw-Hill, 1993.

2. The notion of "scale," and its graphic representation in fractal geometry, is central to the work of the chaos theorists. For a fuller description of what is involved, see Gleick's *Chaos*, p. 83.

3. Kuhn, Thomas. *The Structure of Scientific Revolutions.* Chicago: University of Chicago Press, 1962.

Chapter 3: Chaos, Order, and the Creative Process

1. Korzybski, Alfred. *Science and Sanity,* 5th Edition. Institute of General Semantics, 1995.

2. Additional information on Open Space applications will be found in my book, *Tales from Open Space,* Potomac, MD: Abbott Publishing, 1995. See also *At Work* (Volume 6, Number 2) published by Berrett-Koehler, 1997 and *Peace Corps Tales from Open Space,* U.S. Peace Corps, Information Collection Exchange T0089, 1998. The website of the Open Space Institute <www.openspaceworld.org> is another source.

Chapter 4: The Standard Business Curve Revisited

1. Kübler-Ross, Elisabeth. *On Death and Dying.* New York: Macmillan, 1969.

Chapter 5: Grief at Work

1. Fremantle, Francesca and Trungpa, Chögyan. *The Tibetan Book of the Dead.* Boston, MA: Shambhala, 1987.

Chapter 6: Organization Development in Four Acts

1. Grof, Stanislav. *Beyond the Brain.* Buffalo, NY: State University of New York Press, 1985.

Chapter 7: Stages Along Spirit's Way

1. I owe this nomenclature to Ken Wilbur, who has made a lifetime study of the subject. He has written extensively, but a handy reference to this particular listing may be found in his book, *Up from Eden.* New York: Anchor Press/Doubleday, 1981.

2. Maslow, Abraham. *Religions, Values, and Peak Experiences.* New York: Viking Press, 1970.

3. Charles Wilson, President of General Motors. Quoted in the *New York Times.*

Chapter 8: Over the Edge

1. Pogo, the creation of American cartoonist Walt Kelly, is probably best remembered for his line, "We have met the enemy, and he is us."

2. Reported in the *Washington Post.*

3. The name of the bank is withheld to protect the innocent. I was the facilitator.

Chapter 9: A New Way

1. Buzan, Tony. *The Mind Map Book: How to Use Radiant Thinking to Maximize Your Brain's Untapped Potential.* New York: Plume, 1996.

Chapter 10: Optimization

1. Kelly, Kevin. *Out of Control.* Reading, MA: Addison-Wesley, 1995.

2. Kevin Kelly, author of *Out of Control*, has produced another brilliant piece, *New Rules for the New Economy* (New York: Penguin Books, 1999). The book may be viewed as a first cut "economics of the InterActive Organization." In the New Economy, "freebies" are becoming a way of life.

Chapter 11: Sustaining the Integrity of Spirit

1. Hall, Edward T. *Beyond Culture*. New York: Anchor Press/Doubleday, 1977, p. 16.

2. Owen, H. *Spirit: Transformation and Development in Organizations*. Potomac, MD: Abbott, 1987. This book is now out of print, but the relevant material may be found on my website (www.mindspring.com/~owenhh/). Click on the title, "Papers," then on "Mythos."

3. Sartre, Jean-Paul. *Being and Nothingness*. New York: Washington Square Press, a division of Simon and Schuster, 1956.

4. This story was actually a part of the corporate mythology of a Fortune 500 establishment. The name is withheld for obvious reasons.

5. Bach, Richard. *Jonathan Livingston Seagull*. New York: Macmillan, 1970.

6. Dawkins, Richard. *The Selfish Gene*, Second Edition. Oxford: Oxford University Press, 1989, p. 192.

Chapter 13: Everyday Life in the InterActive Organization

1. Birgitt Bolton is now an independent consultant, but I am sure she would be pleased to tell the story. She may be contacted at birgitt@worldchat.com

Chapter 14: Ethics in the InterActive Organization

1. Junger, Sebastian. *The Perfect Storm: A True Story of Men Against the Sea*. New York: Harper Mass Market, 1998.

SELECTED BIBLIOGRAPHY

Bateson, Gregory. *Steps Towards an Ecology of Mind.* New York: Ballantine, 1972.

Buber, Martin. *I and Thou.* Oxford: T&T Clark, 1937.

Buzan, Tony. *The Mind Map Book: How to Use Radiant Thinking to Maximize Your Brain's Untapped Potential.* New York: Plume, 1996.

Campbell, Jeremy. *Grammatical Man.* New York: Touchstone/Simon and Schuster, 1983.

Campbell, Joseph. *The Masks of God* (in 4 volumes). New York: Viking Press, 1962.

———. *The Hero with a Thousand Faces.* Bolligen Series. Princeton, NJ: Princeton Press, 1949.

Capra, Fritjov. *The Tao of Physics.* New York: Bantam New Age, 1980.

Cassirer, Earnst. *The Philosophy of Symbolic Forms,* Volumes I–IV. New Haven, CT: Yale University Press, 1955.

Collingwood, R.G. *The Idea of History.* Oxford: Oxford University Press, 1946.

Covey, Peter, and Highfield, Roger. *The Frontiers of Complexity.* New York: Fawcett/Columbine, 1996.

Dawkins, Richard. *The Selfish Gene,* Second Edition. Oxford: Oxford University Press, 1989.

Grof, Stanislav. *Beyond the Brain.* Buffalo, NY: State University of New York Press, 1985.

Hall, Edward T. *Beyond Culture.* New York: Anchor Press/Doubleday, 1977.

———. *The Silent Language.* Garden City, NY: Doubleday, 1959.

Heidegger, Martin. *Being and Time*. New York: Harper and Row, 1962.

———. *On the Way to Language*. New York: Harper and Row, 1971.

Jaynes, Julian. *The Origin of Consciousness in the Breakdown of the Bicameral Mind*. Boston, MA: Houghton Mifflin, 1976.

Jung, C.G. *Symbols of Transformation*, Bollingen Series. Princeton, NJ: Princeton University Press, 1956.

Kauffman, Stuart. *At Home in the Universe: The Search for the Laws of Self-Organization and Complexity*. Oxford: Oxford University Press, 1995.

Keirkegaard, Soren. *Philosophical Fragments*. Princeton, NJ: Princeton University Press, 1936.

Kelly, Kevin. *Out of Control: The New Biology of Machines, Social Systems, and the Economic World*. Reading, MA: Addison Wesley, 1995.

———. *New Rules for the New Economy*. New York: Penguin Books, 1999.

Kübler-Ross, Elisabeth. *On Death and Dying*. New York: Macmillan, 1969.

Kuhn, Thomas. *The Structure of Scientific Revolutions*. Chicago: University of Chicago Press, 1962.

Laing, R.D. *The Politics of Experience*. New York: Ballantine Books, 1967.

Langer, Susanne. *Philosophy in a New Key*. Boston, MA: Harvard University Press, 1982.

Lovelock, James. *Gaia: A New Look at Life on Earth*. Oxford: Oxford University Press, 1979.

Mahesh, V.S. *Thresholds of Motivation*. New Delhi: Tata McGraw-Hill, 1993.

Maslow A.H. *Religions, Values, and Peak Experiences*. New York: Viking Press, 1970.

Naisbitt, John. *Megatrends: 10 New Directions Transforming Our Lives*. New York: Warner Books, 1982.

Nielsen, Eduard. *Oral Tradition*. London: SCM Press, 1954.

Pedersen, Johannes. *Israel: Its Life and Culture*. Oxford: Oxford University Press, 1991.

Peters, Tom, and Waterman, Robert H. *In Search of Excellence.* New York: Warner Books, 1981.

Prigogine, Ilya. *Order Out of Chaos.* Toronto: Bantam New Age, 1984.

Russell, Peter. *The Global Brain.* Los Angeles: Tarcher, 1983.

Sartre, Jean-Paul. *Being and Nothingness.* New York: Washington Square Press, a division of Simon and Schuster, 1956.

Tannenbaum, Robert and Hanna, Robert. *Holding On and Letting Go: A Neglected Perspective on Change,* in R. Tannenbaum, N. Margolies, and F. Mazorik, eds., *Human Systems Development.* San Francisco: Jossey-Bass, 1985.

Toffler, Alvin. *The Third Wave.* New York: William Morrow, 1980.

Vaill, Peter. *Towards a Behavioral Description of High Performing Systems,* in Morgan McCall, ed. *Leadership: Where Else Can It Go?* Durham, NC: Duke University Press, 1978.

Wilbur, Ken. *Up From Eden.* New York: Anchor Press/Doubleday, 1981.

———. *Sex, Ecology, and Spirituality.* Boston, MA: Shambhala, 1995.

———. *A Brief History of Everything.* Boston, MA: Shambhala, 1996.

———. *The Eye of Spirit.* Boston, MA: Shambhala, 1997.

———. *The Marriage of Sense and Soul.* New York: Random House, 1998.

Yankelovich, Daniel. *New Rules.* New York: Random House, 1981.

Young, Arthur. *The Reflexive Universe.* New York: Delacorte Press, 1977.

INDEX

ProActive Organizations, 9–10, 100–102, 105–6
  attitude towards chaos, 108
  changes and, 114–17
  community and, 111–13
  isolation, 113–14
  nature of learning, 109
  quality of work and play, 110
  structure and controls, 110–11
  values, 157–58
procedures, 115–16
process, 38, 194
  creative process, 40–45
  of Griefwork, 68–77, 195–96
  security and, 153
productivity, 54, 63, 98, 145, 146
profitability, 63, 98
Promised Land, 19
pubs, 99, 100

Q
questioning, 74–77

R
raplexity, 116
rationalization, 129–30
ReActive Organizations, 9, 96–98
religions, 19–20, 66, 93, 95, 189–90
renewal, 21, 38, 63–64, 66
reorganization, 34–35
research, 120
responsibility, 47, 156
Responsive Organizations, 9, 98–100
resurrection, 66
Robertson, Dale, 182–83

S
Santa Fe Institute, 8, 41, 45
Sartre, Jean-Paul, 161
scale, 28, 216n2
science, 28–29
  physics metaphor, 18–19, 143–44, 161
Scientific Management, 118
search engines, 151
security, 38, 88, 152–55
self-organization, 4, 8–10, 49.
  see also organizations
  healing and, 176–77
  in molecular systems, 41–44
  preconditions, 42, 51–54, 59, 153–54, 194–95
  as reality, 55–56
self-selection, 47, 125
Shiva, 19, 41
shock and anger, 68–70
silence, 73–74
Skunk Works, 128
soul, 93, 102
Soul Pollution, 1–2, 10, 83, 107, 114, 207
space, 1, 159, 161, 163–65.
sparse connections, 43–44, 53, 154, 194
species, 123
Spirit, 7–8. *see also* inspiration
  broken Spirit, 175–76
  ethics and, 201–2
  forms of, 93–95
  line, Spirit, 62, 63
  opening space for, 2–3
  organizational analogue, 95–105
  perceiving, 213–14

V

values, 152, 157–58, 164, 171, 191
   storytelling and, 185–86
Versailles Treaty, 203
Visa International, 128
vision, 77, 85–86
vision statements, 77
void, 66
voluntary self-selection, 47, 125

W

wakes, 72
Wesley Urban Ministry, 183–85
Wilson, Charles, 102
wonder, 76–77
workarounds, 115
work teams, self-managed, 3
work to rule, 116
World War I, 203

Y

Yahweh, 41
yin and yang, 19, 41, 205

ABOUT THE AUTHOR

HARRISON OWEN is president of H. H. Owen and Company. His academic background and training centered on the nature and function of myth, ritual, and culture. In the mid 1960s he left academe to work with a variety of organizations, including small West African villages, urban community organizations (both in the United States and Africa), the Peace Corps, regional medical programs, the U.S. National Institutes of Health, and the U.S. Veterans Administration. Along the way, he discovered that his study of myth, ritual, and culture had direct application to these social systems. In 1977, he created H. H. Owen and Company in order to explore the culture of organizations in transformation as a theorist and practicing consultant. Harrison Owen convened the First International Symposium on Organization Transofrmation and is the originator of Open Space Technology. He is the author of *The Spirit of Leadership: Liberating the Leader in Each of Us; Spirit: Transformation and Development in Organizations; Riding the Tiger; Expanding Our Now: The Story of Open Space Technology; Open Space Technology: A User's Guide; The Millennium Organization;* and *Tales from Open Space.*

Some of Harrison Owen's client engagements and presentations include the following organizations: Owens/Corning Fiberglas, Procter and Gamble, DuPont, Eastern Virginia Medical Authority, Shell/Netherlands, Shell Tankers (Dutch), Shell/Canada, the French Ministry of Telecommunications (PTT), the U.S. Forest Service, the U.S. Internal Revenue Service, Jonathan Corporation, the U.S. Army, Ikea (Sweden), Statoil (Norway), SAS Airlines, Young Presidents Organization, City

University Business School (London), Gronigen University Business School (Holland), Taj Hotel Group (India), Congresso de Desarrollo Organizacional (Mexico), PepsiCola (Venezuela), National Education Association, Toronto-Dominion Bank (Canada) American Management Systems, American Society of Training and Development, Scott Paper, TELCEL/Venezuela, the American Society of Association Executives, the Presbyterian Church (USA), the Accor Hotel Group (France), Ermetek Corp (South Africa), the Union of International Associations (Belgium), Rockport Shoes, Corporate Express, the World Bank, AT&T, IBM, U S WEST, the Organization Development Network, Lucent Technologies, and the Bank of Montreal.